Divisions on a Ground

Northrop Frye

DIVISIONS ON A GROUND

Essays on Canadian Culture

Edited, with a preface, by James Polk

Anansi   Toronto

Cover design: Laurel Angeloff
Author photograph: Roy Nicholls

Published with the assistance of the Canada Council and the Ontario Arts Council, and manufactured in Canada for

House of Anansi Press Limited
35 Britain Street
Toronto, Ontario M5A 1R7

Canadian Cataloguing in Publication Data

Frye, Northrop, 1912-
    Divisions on a Ground: Essays on Canadian Culture

Includes index.

ISBN 0-88784-093-0

1. Canadian literature — Addresses, essays, lectures.
2. Education, Higher — Canada — Addresses, essays,
lectures. 3. Canada — Civilization — Addresses,
essays, lectures. I. Title.

FC95.4.F79   971   C82-094105-0
F1021.2.F79

1 2 3 4 5 / 89 88 87 86 85 84 83 82

Printed and bound in Canada by
T. H. Best Printing Company Limited

Divisions on a Ground

Contents

Editor's Preface

I have grouped these essays into three sections—on writing, the university, and the social good—well aware that such tidy packaging runs counter to the very spirit of Northrop Frye's critical approach, which supposes a fluid interaction between the arts and society. I can only hope that my arrangement may emphasize the range of Frye's inquiry into his own country, which is by no means restricted to the sighting of a Canadian literature, important as he has been there. Frye has been explaining Canada to itself for over four decades, while also working in the field as a teacher and administrator and serving on the task forces, committees and commissions with which a society rewards its best minds. During this time, his views on Canada have remained steady, particularly his faith that there is a literature of consequence and a country to match. Of course, over the years, there have been modulations and key changes in these insights, and it is fascinating to watch the ideas Frye formulated in the essays of the 1940s and 50s evolve and exfoliate in his later essays from the 60s and 70s which are collected here. Thus the title for this volume, *Divisions on a Ground*, lifted from music, in which a "ground" or a ground bass sounds a theme which is repeated as the "divisions" or variations in the other voices take off in startling and provocative ways.

The title may also bring to mind Canada's geographical ground and the mapmaker's divisions which give us our shaping silhouette. Frye has often emphasized the importance of Canada's physical land-mass, noting that its empty spaces encourage a suspicion of nature and a "garrison mentality" in our cultural outlook. In the pieces collected here, he continues to explore Canadian space, pointing out, for example, that not only does it prompt a certain sobriety in our nature poetry, but that it also explains our bias for communications and communications theorists. In essays from the 1950s, collected in *The Bush Garden (1971)*, he suggested that regionalism gave a special vitality to the work of, say, E.J. Pratt and Earle Birney; in later essays he can still point to the force of the regional in, say, Jack Hodgins, or Susan Musgrave, or Rudy Wiebe. In 1965, he suggested, in the "Conclusion" to the *Literary History of Canada*, that the Canadian writer's overwhelming question was not so much "Who am I?" as "Where is Here?"; in the revised "Conclusion" of 1976, reprinted here, he comments on the complex ways in which newer writers have tried to answer both questions, and throws out some unexpected variations about comedy in Canada, about literature as "play", about the United States becoming Canadianized.

Frye's pleasure in the flowering of Canadian letters makes this section of *Divisions on a Ground* extremely agreeable reading. Whatever is made of his interpretation of our literature (some, for example, see him as a romantic populist, others as a mandarin elitist: there seems to be plenty of scope for discussion), even the most ungrateful critic could not deny his role in the development of Canada's writing or his influence on writers. His insights into the university have been less celebrated, perhaps because his adamant belief in the importance of teaching the humanities has been voiced more often to the academic community than to the public at large. Certainly, it is no blind and foolish idealism. Frye has taught at the University of Toronto since the dawn of time (1937), and knows full well that most incoming freshmen will be unacquainted with anything remotely resembling a good book, much less a literary tradition. He is aware that a great deal of scholarship is, or may seem, frivolous and self-serving. He is alert to the student rebellion of the 60s and to the plight of the unemployed PhD. of the 70s graduating into the taxicab business or the breadline. He is hugely entertaining about the less savory aspects of the Modern

Languages Association Convention—and yet, his speech to that organization ends with a thumping affirmation of humanistic values and the idea of the university. Some details in this middle section may seem dated: at least, the New Left student is gone with the dinosaur, and the *Esquire* girl lolls no more in the pages of that magazine. I thought of cutting these things out, but they help to locate us in time, and anyway, Frye's genius for isolating the central pattern of a thing — whether it be in Blake, the Bible or the ways of the Budget Committee — keeps the ideas fresh and durable. Here, as everywhere, he is our most practical critic.

I stress this, because there are still those who regard Frye as some sort of ivory-tower cosmologist remote from the concerns of everyday reading and living. Frye himself has protested this view (in the preface, for example, to *The Critical Path*), and every essay in this book displays his profound concern for the society in which art is made, for the citizen for whom art is meant. In the last section, especially, I've gathered essays and addresses in which Frye most openly speculates on social and metaphysical issues, although all of his literary criticism is relevant. He discusses, among other things, the meaning of Canadian history, the racking speed of social change and future shock, the meaning of tradition, the meaning of life. Nothing less. In the final, beautiful address in this book, he dares to talk about his own approaches to living in the 20th Century—a risky business for a literary critic, or for anyone else—and is, I think precise, sympathetic and useful, speaking directly and clearly to a large audience. I can't imagine another critic who would do this, or one who could.

Approximately half of the pieces in this book, in fact, were designed as public speeches, offering us the chance of listening to a major literary theorist at his most relaxed and congenial. *Divisions on a Ground* seems to me a good place to start reading Frye, especially if one has been scared off by his reputation for difficulty. I should note that I have cut certain opening remarks in the speeches which seemed too topical or too "occasional" for a book. I have also blue-pencilled some paragraphs where Frye necessarily repeats the same literary examples from essay to essay, and have invented a few titles to keep the word "culture" from tolling too often through the Table of Contents. All of the original titles and bibliographical data are noted at the back of the book. Other than that, the editor of Northrop Frye is left with little enough to do: the essays are models of purposeful structuring, the prose is immaculate. The spelling is correct. For help at every step of the way, I was aided with great kindness by Professor Frye, by his research assistant, Michael Dolzani, and by his invaluable secretary, Jane Widdicombe. All are blameless; the faults are mine.

What, finally, does a major critic, perhaps the most important in our century, make of the country he inhabits and its culture? The reader will decide, but it seems to me that Frye's vision of Canada in its present incarnation is quite cheering. If salvation lies in the word, then Frye reports to us that our literature is now one "of extraordinary vigour and historical significance". He is quick to add that such a blessed state may not last long and that the media blitz from the south may one day flatten all cultural distinction. Everywhere rapture is modified: caution, as Frye himself has underlined, remains an identifying feature of the national temperament. Yet things could be worse. Our schools and institutions, however riddled with flaws, remain, and, in some instances, prevail. Frye is very far from proclaiming the New Jerusalem, but the reader may sense, as I do, his pleased relief in contemplating the culture he supported so cogently in the 40s and 50s, decades when he rejoiced in Canada's achievements but might reasonably have wished for a closer correlation between his faith and the nation's works. Now, with a robust literature at hand and Northrop Frye as witness, we might be excused for believing ourselves in a springtime or a high summer of cultural growth. Clearly Frye's own writing and thinking is part of this fortunate cycle, and the proof can be found in the divisions on the following pages.

James Polk
Anansi

I
Writing

Culture as Interpenetration

As long as I have been a literary critic, I have been interested in the relations between a culture and the social conditions under which it is produced. It has always puzzled me why so little seems to be known about this, when so much work, even so much first-rate work, has been done in what seem to be all the relevant areas. I have also been watching the Canadian cultural scene for about forty years, and I feel that Canada is perhaps as interesting and valuable a place as any to study such a question. What follows is a series of observations that might conceivably lead to some more general principles on the subject. I am confining the term culture, because of limited space, to the creative arts, and to painting and literature within those arts.

There is an aged and now somewhat infirm joke to the effect that the United States has passed from barbarism to decadence without an intervening period of civilization. A parallel and possibly more accurate statement might be made of Canada: that it has passed from a pre-national to a post-national phase without ever having become a nation. It very nearly became one in the two decades following the second World War, when it took an active part in international politics, acquired a national flag, and was for a time a perceptible military and naval power. But it never shook off its role as an American satellite sufficiently to be taken very seriously as a distinctive political presence even then. As third-world nations began to emerge in Africa and Asia, Canada's much more low-keyed nationalism became increasingly inaudible, like a lute in a brass band. Two books with highly significant titles appeared at the beginning and end respectively of this period: A.R.M. Lower's *Colony to Nation* in 1946 and George Grant's *Lament for a Nation* in 1965. When Trudeau became prime minister and adopted Marshall McLuhan as one of his advisors, Canada reverted to tribalism.

The settlement of America was a centrifugal movement out from Britain and France, and to centralize is to create a hierarchy. The top of the hierarchy is the central city, London or Paris, which is where all the cultural action is. In Elizabethan England, for example, literary culture was a London culture. If a writer were upper class, he would write Petrarchan love lyrics and send them around to his friends in manuscript, prior to arranging for a publisher to steal them. If he were middle class, he would turn to the theatre or to pamphleteering. But *qua* writer he could hardly live or work for long outside London: one thinks of Herrick, for instance, a parson stuck in Devonshire, writing nostalgically of jewellery, perfume, women's clothes, and his happy times with the "tribe of Ben". This situation lasted until late in the eighteenth century. Wordsworth was the first major English writer to set up his headquarters outside London, and of course by Victorian times, with the rise of the great Midland cities, the cultural picture was quite different. In France, with its more limited industrial development, culture remained fixated on Paris for a much longer time. As late as my own student days, I remember seeing in Paris an exhibition of a sculptor who lived in (I think) Dijon, advertised under the slogan "France is not Paris".

Discussions about Canadian literature began, in English Canada, about a hundred years ago, when it was still uncertain whether the condition was one of genuine pregnancy or merely wind. At that time the commonest argument advanced was that in a young and newly settled country the priorities were material ones, and that literature and the other arts would come along when economic conditions were more advanced. This argument makes very little sense: in a genuinely primitive community, like that of the Eskimos, where food and shelter are requirements that have constantly to be met, poetry (and other arts, such as carving) leaps into the foreground as one of the really essential elements of life. Something similar may be true of new societies that are not primitive: seventeenth-century Puritans in Massachusetts wrote poetry and carried on with their pamphlet war against the Anglican establishment. It is also possible, in modern times, for the centrifugal movement from the main centres to reverse itself, for works of culture to be export goods coming out of a small community. One thinks of the amount of Anglo-Irish literature produced in the last century, which was certainly never intended for the Dublin market.

No: Canadian assumptions about the low and late priority of creative activity were mercantilist assumptions, and signified the acquiescence by Canadians in their role as producers of raw materials for manufacturing centres outside Canada. What got the priority were the engineering modes of communication, the fantastically long and expensive railways, bridges and canals that sprouted out of the nineteenth-century Canadian landscape. It was no more natural for Canada to produce such things than to produce major developments in literature or painting, but they were produced because they fitted the premises of Canadian mythology at that time. But while the prevailing mood was one of expansion into a bountiful future, other directions were indicated by the turn of the century, when the Boer War was fought. In the first World War there was a patriotic picture called "Canada's Answer", depicting battleships on the ocean. The point of the picture was, of course, Canada's willingness to defend the mother country by sending soldiers over the sea. But the subject of the picture was again an engineering mode of communication, except that this time it was associated with a feeling that the noblest destiny for a human Canadian life was to become a sacrificial object in a European war. The assumptions here are getting a little more sinister than the purely mercantilist ones, and need more looking into.

One of the most remarkable works of fiction in our time, Thomas Pynchon's *Gravity's Rainbow*, suggests that the human instinct to see humanly intelligible pattern and design in nature is a form of paranoia. That is, man cannot endure the thought of an environment that was not made primarily for his benefit, or, at any rate, made without reference to his own need to see order in it. Man describes his total environment as a "universe"; something that all turns around one centre, though often mentally suppressing the fact that that centre is himself. He clings to the argument of design as long as he can, projecting the notion of a man-related universe on God: when he is forced to give that up, he plunges into a mathematical order, the animated algebra of technology. As he goes on, it becomes increasingly clear that his "rage for order", in Stevens' phrase, is linked to a death-wish — Pynchon's symbol for it is the V-2 rocket bomb of the second World War.

However, to live without the sense of a need for order, Pynchon suggests, requires an inhuman detachment that is not possible nor perhaps desirable. What fights effectively against the destructive impulse can only be a "counterforce" or creative paranoia, a unifying power that works towards life and the fulfilment of desire instead of towards death. Such a creative force would naturally be closely allied to the work of the dream. Freud, in the *Traumdeutung*, remarks more than once on the curious compulsion in the dream work to unify a great variety of disparate experiences and themes. For Pynchon the opposite of this creative drama, the anti-dream, so to speak, is Kekulé's famous dream of the ouroboros that turned into the benzene ring, and thereby inaugurated a new and deadly era of technology. There are other vivid episodes in the book making the same point. We are told of a madman who exterminated the dodoes in Mauritius because, being awkward and unadaptable, they seemed to him an offence against the argument for design. This modulates to a hideous picture of the formerly German colony of Southwest Africa, where the native population was slaughtered to the verge of extinction out of the bloodthirsty superstition known as social Darwinism, the belief that some people are better fitted to survive than others because they possess greater powers of destruction. It seems to me that this argument in *Gravity's Rainbow* affords an instructive parallel to some of the social conditions underlying Canadian literature.

New France and New England were colonized in the Baroque phase of European development. Certain religious and philosophical assumptions that they brought with them explain a good many features of that colonization. Let us take the religious ones first. Christianity is a revolutionary and urban religion, and, like Marxism in our day, it started with all the revolutionary characteristics: the belief in a specific historical revelation, a canon of sacred texts, an obsession with the dangers of heresy, and, above all, a dialectical habit of mind, a tendency to polarize everything into the for and the against. Such an attitude is by no means essential to a religion. When Buddhism came to Japan it collided with the indigenous Shinto cult, and after a good deal of tension, a Buddhist theologian suggested that the *kami*, the gods and nature-spirits of Shinto, could be thought of as emanations of the Buddha: in short, that Shintoism could be regarded as a positive analogy of Buddhism. As a result the two religions have co-existed in Japan ever since. But for Christianity, as for Islam and Marxism later, nothing will go right until the entire world is united in the right creed, and whatever place there may be in Christian thought for natural religion, no non-Christian faith can ever be anything but a negative analogy, a demonic parody, of Christianity. And when even saints and martyrs firmly believe that the only good heathenism is a dead heathenism, it becomes very easy for others to infer that the only good heathen is a dead heathen. What is particularly horrifying about the extinction of, say, the Beothuks in Newfoundland is the casualness with which it was done, the ability to murder people of a different ethnical group without losing five minutes' sleep over it. It is rather curious that the Eichmann trial of a few years ago should have come to so many people as a shocking discovery.

The differences between the Puritan Protestantism of New England and the Jansenist Catholicism of New France are of very little importance here. Both felt equally that there could be no truck with any nature-spirits or with any sense of identity between human and animal life, such as we have in some aspects of totemism. The horror of idolatry, the feeling that there could be nothing numinous in nature and that all the spiritual beings man had discovered in nature were really devils, was deeply rooted in Christianity, as was the feeling that man had to depend solely on human and social institutions for any improvement in his status. Nature became therefore an unrestricted area for human exploitation. God had said to Noah after the flood, at the very beginning of history: "The fear of you and the dread of you shall be upon every beast of the earth . . . into your hand are they delivered". Hence the savage and superstitious custom of apologizing to the spirits of the fish or the deer and explaining that their human hunters were taking only enough for their own food was replaced by the enlightened and civilized custom of slaughtering everything in sight until one species after another disappeared from the earth forever.

Such traditional tendencies had been increased by the Baroque sense, most articulate in Descartes, that the consciousness of man created an immense gap between him and all other living creatures, who belonged primarily in a world of mechanism. The newly discovered power of mathematics, too, was at its clearest at the exploring and pioneering periphery of Baroque culture, in the astrolabes and compasses that guided the explorer, in the grid-patterns that eventually were imposed on city and country alike. Every "improvement" in communication since then, in railway, highway, or airway, has meant a shorter and straighter path through nature until, with the plane, the sense of moving through nature practically disappears. What does not disappear is the attitude of arrogant ascendancy over nature. For the white conquerors of this continent, creation does not begin with an earth-mother who is the womb and tomb of all created things, but with a sky-father who planned and ordered and made the world, in a tour de force of technology. The despoiling of nature has now reached the point at which the white settlement of America begins to look like a very clear example of what Pynchon means by his death-wish paranoia, a destructiveness increasing in efficiency and ferocity until it finally began to turn on itself.

Baroque Christianity still maintained the rigidly authoritarian world-picture inherited from medieval times, in which there is a downward movement from God to man and an upward movement from man towards God. For a natural religion like that of most of the native peoples, evil, suffering and above all death do not cause a problem: death belongs in the cycle of nature from the beginning. But for a religion thinking in terms of an omniscient God planning and making the world, the world as originally made could not have had any evil or death in it, and hence a myth of fall was necessary to account for the contrast between the model world that God must have made and the actual world that surrounds us. The gap caused by the fall was closed by the Incarnation, when a principle of authority descended from the divine world to the human one. This principle of authority continues in the church and in the secular power focussed in the monarchy.

Man's response to divine authority is to raise his status from the lower nature into which he fell to the higher nature symbolized by the garden of Eden. But he can do this only through unswerving obedience to the sacraments of the church, the principles of morality, and the canons of secular law. Once again, there is no significant difference on this point between the Quebec Catholic and the Massachusetts Puritan. The Puritans were revolutionaries, but not for liberal or democratic reasons: they looked forward to a rule of the elect in which, to paraphrase Paul, the powers that be would not be ordained *of* God for man's sins, but ordained *by* God for his redemption.

The first white man to write poetry in what is now Canada, Marc Lescarbot, wrote a poem in 1606 addressed to some Frenchmen returning to France from Port Royal. He says (in F.R. Scott's translation):

> 'Tis you who go to see congenial friends
> In language, habits, customs and religion
> And all the lovely scenes of your own nation,
> While we among the savages are lost
> And dwell bewildered on this clammy coast.

Then he pulls himself together and speaks of what may yet be made of the country, after, perhaps, missionaries will have come

> And bring conversion to this savage nation
> That has no God, no laws and no religion.

Lescarbot thus defines a kind of cultural primal scene for Canada. In front of him, as he gazes wistfully at it, is the ship going back to rejoin the centre of culture and good life in France. Behind him is the great gap in existence, like one of the black holes of modern astronomy, created by the indigenous people — that is, of course, created by his view of them. We notice how the cultural situation exactly fits the religious and political one. In culture, as in religion and politics, the homeland is the source of authority, and the first duty of a colonial culture is to respond to it.

Lescarbot's verses inaugurate the first period of Canadian culture, the uncomplicated provincial or colonial period. One may distinguish three main phases in its development. In the first phase the provincial culture tends to imitate externally rather than by absorption, accepting certain standards and trying to meet them. It confines its attention to what is established in the home-land and has become a principle of cultural authority there. It is obvious that cultural lag is built in to such a process. In poetry of the Confederation period and earlier, while the ostensible echoes may be from Tennyson or Victor Hugo, the actual texture of the verse is usually closer to James Thomson or Béranger. Such external imitation is a self-defeating enterprise because a writer cannot meet external standards, but can only establish his own. Gradually, however, the first phase evolves into the second phase. The more mature colonial writing gets, the more contemporary the influences become: the writer has got out of the schoolroom and has joined a community. It is still a mercantilist situation, but some initiative has gone into the provincial manufactures.

These two phases represent different and contrasting ways of dealing with a sense of urgency connected with content, with a need to grapple directly with the new stimuli and situations encountered in a new land. Content is often regarded, even by artists themselves, as dictating its own forms, but this is an ele-mentary fallacy: the forms of every art are generated from within the art. In the first phase it is obscurely felt that the more tradi-tional the form, the better adapted it is to containing the new experience. The second phase swings to the opposite extreme and assumes that only the latest models are equipped to do the same job.

Poetry in Canada did not fare very well under these imitative phases, although naturally we can see a steady maturing process going on as, in English, pre-Raphaelite formulas are replaced by the influence of Eliot and the later Yeats, and, in French, a good deal of yawny verse about the *terroir* gives way to livelier echoes of Paul Fort and Claudel. Fiction was even more retarded. Painting is by far the most interesting art in Canada up to about 1960. Here the urgency of new content could find its place in a remarkable docu-mentary development, which begins with the military and exploring painting of the age of Paul Kane and Thomas Davies, and continues through Thomson and the Group of Seven in Ontario, along with Emily Carr in British Columbia and a number of painters in Quebec. It is often said that these later groups broke with stale pictorial conventions and began to look directly at the country in front of them. There clearly must be some truth in this, as I have said it myself: however, the fallacy of content shaping form lurks within it. The lapse of time brings with it a decreasing attention to subject-matter and an increasing awareness of convention. It is this lapse of time that makes us more conscious of the Barbazon and Dutch pastoral influences on the older landscape painters, and the continuing of the lapse that turns our interest from the "solemn land" of northern Ontario as painted by Thomson and MacDonald towards the fauve and art nouveau conventions that controlled their vision of it.

The final phase, in which provincial culture becomes fully mature, occurs when the artist enters into the cultural heritage that his predecessors have drawn from, and paints or writes without any sense of a criterion external to himself and his public. Here the anxieties about meeting proper standards or being up to date or expressing a distinctive subject-matter with enough emphasis (or what was once called, in connection with Hemingway, false hair on the chest) have all disappeared. While I was reviewing English Canadian poetry during the fifties, I noticed how many of the best people were turning erudite, allusive, even academic. I felt that this indicated the growth of an unforced and relaxed sense of a cultural tradition, one which could now be absorbed instead of merely imitated or echoed. Of course all the anxieties listed above were still in the air, and I was widely regarded as encouraging a new form of inhibited provincialism. But what I saw in, for example, Leonard Cohen's *Let Us Compare Mythologies*, Jay Macpherson's *The Boatman*, Margaret Avison's *Winter Sun*, James Reaney's *Suit of Nettles* seemed to me an attitude to cultural tradition that looked forward rather than back.

In 1952 some people in a small town in Ontario, simply because it was called Stratford, decided to put on some Shakespeare, and a Shakespeare festival began there the next year. The director was Tyrone Guthrie and the leading actors were Alec Guinness and Irene Worth — not precisely what the CRTC would call Canadian content. Those who think in pigeonholes could hardly point to anything more obviously parochial and colonial. Yet there are three factors to be considered. First, the beginning of the Shakespeare festival at Stratford turned out to be a very important event in the history of *Canadian* drama: it helped to foster a school of Canadian actors, and the lift in morale it represented fostered Canadian playwriting as well. Second, it represented an extraordinary recreation of the power and freshness of

Shakespeare himself: one almost felt sorry for the British, who, having no Stratford except the one that had actually produced Shakespeare, would find it harder to make this kind of rediscovery of him. And third, Shakespeare at Stratford does not stand alone, because Molière played a very similar role in the development of French Canadian drama, at roughly the same time.

In proportion as Canada shook off its external and sub-ordinating assumptions about its English and French cultural heritages, the genuine form of cultural development became more obvious. This genuine form is what I mean by interpenetration. As Shelley demonstrated in his *Defence of Poetry*, the language of the creative imagination is a language that cannot argue: it is not based on propositions that do battle with their implied opposites. What it does is to create a vision that becomes a focus for a community. This means that it has, at least at the beginning, a limited range. Shelley himself, writing in a culture that had been London-dominated for a thousand years, suggests (in his preface to *Prometheus Unbound*) that for the best future developments in culture England should break down into about forty republics, each with a central city about the size of Periclean Athens or Medicean Florence.

Shelley was writing at a time when there was a strong liberal sympathy with self-determinism of nations as opposed to empires, with Italy against the Austrian empire, with Greece against the Turkish one. Since then it has become increasingly obvious that political and economic organization tends to centralize and unify. But Shelley seems to be right about cultural matters. Literature and painting do appear to depend on decentralization in a very subtle way. The artist seems to draw strength from a very limited community: American writers, for instance, generally turn out, under closer analysis, to be southern writers, New England writers, expatriate writers, New York writers, and so on. They need a certain cultural coherence within their community, but the community itself is not their market. This is where the principle of interpenetration operates: the more intensely Faulkner concentrates on his unpronounceable county in Mississippi, the more intelligible he becomes to readers all over the world.

We are back to the question of the challenge of content. Contemporary painting and writing, whatever the language, speaks an international idiom, and the capitals where that idiom is established are still, as they have always been, the big centres, London, Paris, New York. Trying to ignore this international idiom is, experience suggests, futile, and leads only to a kind of archaism. The general principle appears to be that a painter or writer who is self-conscious about his immediate context will be likely to sound provincial, whereas a painter or writer who accepts a provincial milieu, in, say, Newfoundland or southern British Columbia, will be much less likely to do so. A Canadian artist may leave Canada to live and work in one of the big centres, like the painter Riopelle, but this does not affect the matter. Within the last twenty years we have been seeing more and more areas of this huge and sparsely settled country become culturally visible through painters and writers who belong, as creative people, less to Canada than to the prairies, the Pacific coast, the Atlantic coast, southern Ontario or Quebec. The process has been aided by Canada's more relaxed attitude to ethnical groups: there is no such thing as a hundred per cent Canadian, and the homogenizing of immigrants has been less intense than in the United States. But if we look at the pictures of Kurelek on the prairies or Jack Chambers in Ontario, or read Buckler on the Maritimes or Rudy Wiebe on Alberta Mennonites, we can see the "provincial" aspect of Canadian culture going into reverse, from inarticulate form to articulate content.

Across the River
and Out of the Trees

The first issue of the *University of Toronto Quarterly* appeared in 1931. Its appearance was not exactly a breathtaking novelty: *Queen's Quarterly* and the *Dalhousie Review* were already in existence, and there had even been an earlier version of the *Quarterly* itself. But it was an important historical event none the less. The opening editorial statement attached the journal's traditions firmly to those of the "gentleman's magazine" of the eighteenth and nineteenth centuries. It was *not* to be a specialized learned journal: there were already enough of those, the editor implied, perhaps meaning that there were too many. Nor was it to be an outlet for creative talent in poetry or fiction: it published a poem or two at the beginning, but apologized editorially for the digression. It tried to cover a broad spectrum of academic interest for a while, but soon restricted itself in effect to the humanities, though it did not acknowledge this by called itself a "Journal of the Humanities" until some years later. Within a very short time it had inaugurated "Letters in Canada" as an encyclopaedic critique of everything published in Canada, so for all its exclusion of poetry and fiction it clearly had no intention of slighting the Canadian cultural scene, much less ignoring it.

There were some remarkable people first associated with the journal. There was G.S. Brett, the first editor, a philosopher of vast erudition whose *History of Psychology* is still a standard work on the subject. There was E.K. Broadus, one of an extraordinary group of scholars in Alberta, and an early Canadian anthologist. There was Pelham Edgar, interested mainly in what was then contemporary fiction, author of a pioneering work on Henry James, and deeply concerned with Canadian writing as well. There was E.K. Brown, whose book on Canadian poetry was crucial in consolidating the sense of the context and tone of Canadian poetry up to that time. There was Watson Kirkconnell, whose prolific output and fantastic linguistic abilities enabled "Letters in Canada" to include a survey of Canadian writing in languages other than English and French, all of which he could read. A malicious but admiring legend said that when he became President of Acadia he took to shaking hands with his left hand so as not to interrupt his writing. An early issue contained an article by Kirkconnell on "Canada's Leading Poet," who according to Kirkconnell was Stephan Stephansson, a poet living in Manitoba and writing in Icelandic up to his death in 1927.

I was preoccupied with getting through my sophomore year when the *Quarterly* first appeared, and I should perhaps not have been aware of its existence for some time if Brett and Edgar had not been teachers of mine. If I adopt a personal, even to some extent an autobiographical, tone in what follows, the reason is not simple egotism or garrulity: one needs a point of view for a survey, and a personal point of view is the obvious one for a surveyor who has lived entirely within the territory he surveys. In retrospect, the *Quarterly*'s early editorial policy decisions seem to me to have been prophetic of my own interests in criticism, and objectified much of what I have tried to do since. They also seem to me to mark a most significant cultural change, which was among other things a change in the university's relation to society, and which was already taking place, in Canada as elsewhere.

The learned journals the *UTQ* was separating itself from belonged mainly to the philological tradition, with its head-quarters in nineteenth-century Germany, that had dominated American scholarship for half a century. The scholars who wrote in them generally knew the standard classical and modern languages, and for the most part did not include contemporary literature in their purview — at least not as scholars, whatever their general level of cultivation. Their scholarship thus gave the impression of being an activity independent of the creative life of their time. This was particularly true of Canadian scholars in 1930, many of whom had not only moved to Canada from elsewhere but had done much of their seminal work before they arrived. But the number of university people who gathered around *The Canadian Forum*, established in 1920, indicated that other things were happening.

My own college of Victoria had produced a monument of philological scholarship, Andrew Bell's *The Latin Dual and Poetic Diction* (1923), a work so obsessively specialized that the Classicists themselves hardly knew what to do with it. Yet the genial and urbane scholarship of Douglas Bush, another graduate of Victoria, who in his early years was a lively contributor to *The Canadian Forum*, grew directly out of this environment. Edgar's contemporary interests I have noted: he also influenced Brown's interest in twentieth-century American and Canadian writing, besides getting E.J. Pratt into his own English department at Victoria. Pratt was not a "writer in residence," but a full-time teacher until his retirement, and all the more influential as a link between creative and scholarly interests for both students and colleagues. He was a portent of the modern university's acceptance of some responsibility for encouraging writers and fostering a discriminating public for them.

In 1930 Canadian literature was still in a provincial state. Pratt and Morley Callaghan had established themselves as twentieth-century writers, and in 1936 a little anthology of six poets, including Pratt, called *New Provinces*, indicated that newer and more contemporary poetic idioms were taking shape. Morley Callaghan's books, I think I am right in saying, were sometimes banned by the public library in Toronto — I forget what the rationalization was, but the real reason could only have been that if a Canadian were to do anything so ethically dubious as write, he should at least write like a proper colonial and not like someone who had lived in the Paris of Joyce and Gertrude Stein. More recent scholarship has revealed that there was a good deal of remarkable, even astonishing, writing produced in Canada before 1930, but a mass of writing with good flashes in it is still not a literature. Articles proclaiming the imminent advent of literary greatness had been appearing for a long time, giving to Canadian literature, or its history, the quality that Milton Wilson has described, in a practically definitive phrase, as "one half-baked phoenix after another."

The excuse normally given for this state of affairs was that Canada was a "young" country, that its priorities had to be material ones, and that literature and the other arts would come along when economic conditions were more advanced. First the primary forms of communication, railways, bridges, canals, then the secondary ones. This argument makes very little sense: seventeenth-century Puritans in Massachusetts wrote poetry and carried on with their pamphlet war against the Anglican establishment. And in a genuinely primitive community, like those of the indigenous peoples, poetry leaps into the foreground as one of the really essential elements of life, along with food and shelter. It was no more "natural", and no more in accord with the historical process, for Canada to build the Victoria Bridge or the Welland Canal than to have produced major poets and novelists. But the argument was accepted because it was a mercantilist argument, and was part of Canada's acceptance of its role as a provider of raw materials for manufacture in larger centres. The reverse movement of imported goods brought the standards of culture set up in London and Paris back to the boondocks, and efforts were made there to imitate them.

In 1930, again, the depression settled into Canadian life, and the depression was also a hampering and delaying influence on culture. There was not only the difficulty of getting books and pictures marketed (A.Y. Jackson remarked to me some time before his death that he still had guilt feelings when a picture of his sold for more than thirty-five dollars), but a theory of culture developed which was a modified form of mercantilism. According to it the creative person was to produce the raw material of his experience as part of an attempt to affect the ownership of production. There has always been a strong realistic and documentary slant to Canadian writing and painting, for obvious reasons, and this stereotype, after confusing a number of writers and spoiling one or two quite decent painters, hung around for several decades, though it shifted to a more psychological basis in the fifties. Clearly this was still another way of reducing literature to rhetoric, and focussing attention on content, or what a writer thinks he is saying, rather than on what he constructs, or says in spite of himself.

When I was reviewing Canadian poetry in the fifties, I noted the emergence of a curiously interconsistent language of symbolism and imagery among the poets who most obviously knew what they were doing. The language had close affiliations with that of contemporary British and American poets, but was a quite distinctive language, a direct response, as I felt, to an environment that was taking on a new significance for them. I have spoken of what I call a garrison mentality and of the alternating moods of pastoral populism and imaginative terror (which has nothing to do with a poet's feeling terrified) in earlier Canadian writing. These were set up mainly as historical markers, like roadside plaques telling a motorist that something happened here two centuries ago, but they also attempted to define elements in a cultural tradition that was taking clearer shape as the contemporary writing matured. For those who felt that a poet ought primarily to express either sexual passion or social indignation, and was doing so if he said he was loudly enough, my comments on the emergence of a new variety of symbolic language sounded like a preference for poetry that was academic and inhibited. I myself felt that a quality was forming in Canadian poetry that I could only call professional. I finished my survey in 1960 convinced that Canadian literature was about to become a phoenix again, and a properly cooked one this time.

Well, I think I was right: Canadian literature since 1960 has become a real literature, and is recognized as one all over the world. We are told that there are Canadian authors who sell better in Holland or Germany than they do in their own country — and it has never been fair to say that the Canadian public has ignored its own literature, as far as buying and reading books goes. I doubt if there are any real causes for such a development, but there are some obvious conditioning factors. The Massey Report, published in 1951, was a landmark in the history of Canadian culture, not merely because it recommended a Canada Council, but because it signified the end of cultural *laissez faire* and assumed that the country itself had a responsibility for fostering its own culture. Back in 1930, Pelham Edgar was trying to organize voluntary societies for the relief of indigent authors, and there was an all too

frequent assumption that society should concern itself with literature only when it felt like denouncing or censoring it. But the
principle of social responsibility was established with the Massey
Report, and without that principle Canadian literature would
perhaps still be in its nonage. Federal support has been supplemented in the wealthier provinces, to the advantage of all
concerned.

In his book *Odysseus Ever Returning* George Woodcock
quotes a review by Oscar Wilde in which Wilde praises an
American writer for being concerned with the literature he loves
rather than the country in which he lives, adding "the Muses care
so little for geography". As usual, Wilde's critical instinct is
sound: a writer cannot try to be anything except a writer, and a
poet must adhere to literature, which is where his technical equip-
ment comes from, not to the false rhetoric of the factitious and the
voulu. But the last comment seems to me dead wrong. No Muse
can function outside human space and time, that is, outside
geography and history. Wilde himself owed his whole being as a
writer to the tiny area of Anglo-Irish ascendancy which provided
his own space and time. So while a Canadian writer may go anywhere and make any sort of statement about the place of Canada in
his life, positive or negative, his formative environment and his
ability as a writer will be interdependent, however different. Our
knowledge of "Canada" is inferred from what, for example, Jack
Hodgins tells us about Vancouver Island or Robertson Davies
about southwestern Ontario or Roger Lemelin about the *pente
douce* in Quebec City. A writer working outside Canada, like
Mavis Gallant, is evidence that Canadian literature is diversified
enough to have its expatriates as well, as American literature had
its T.S. Eliot and Gertrude Stein.

In an "instant world" of communication, there is no reason
for cultural lag or for a difference between sophisticated writers in
large centres and naive writers in smaller ones. A world like ours
produces a single international style of which all existing litera-
tures are regional developments. This international style is not a
bag of rhetorical tricks but a way of seeing and thinking in a world
controlled by uniform patterns of technology, and the regional
development is a way of escaping from that uniformity. If we read,
say, Wilson Harris's *Palace of the Peacock* and then Robert
Kroetsch's *Badlands* one after the other, we find that there is no

similarity between them, and that one story is steeped in Guyana and the other in Alberta. But certain structural affinities, such as the fold over in time, indicate that they are both products of much the same phase of cultural development.

II

In 1930 native Canadian scholarship in the humanities was, as suggested above, spotty, and in a state of uneasy transition from nineteenth- to twentieth-century conceptions of humanism. Within the next twenty years a remarkable change had taken place. In 1950 I had a year off on a Guggenheim Fellowship and went to Harvard, and on my first visit to the bookstores I was startled at the prominence in them of books by my colleagues at home. I knew about the books, naturally, but seeing them in that context was a different experience. There were Cochrane's great book on Christianity and Classical culture, Barker Fairley's second book on Goethe, Kathleen Coburn's edition of Coleridge's *Philosophical Lectures*, F.E.L. Priestley's edition of Godwin's *Political Justice*, my own book on Blake, Woodhouse's edition of the Clark Papers with its epoch-making introduction, Arthur Barker's book on Milton and Puritanism, still standard after nearly forty years — there were several others, but I remember seeing those. Not a bad showing, I thought, for Canadian scholarship with its very inadequate libraries and travel grants (I am speaking of 1950). There were other signs too, like the establishment of the Pontifical Institute of Medieval Studies under Gilson, which indicated that Canadian scholarship in the humanities had become a genuine presence in the world. The scholarship had come to maturity rather earlier than the literature, and the fact nagged my subconscious for the next decade.

The expansion of scholarly activity represented by the setting up of the "Letters in Canada" column of *University of Toronto Quarterly* meant that some scholarship, at least, was becoming assimilated to reviewing, even to journalism. And this kind of criticism has been traditionally regarded as a subordinate, even a parasitic activity. It was recognized that writers needed honest and informed criticism, but such criticism was the blest office of the epicene, of the bee who carries the pollen for the flower but does not fertilize it himself. I felt that when criticism and scholarship were the same activity (and an academic critic surely ought to apply the same principles to whatever he writes about) this parasitic relation to the writer disappeared. The academic critic is primarily concerned with the expansion of knowledge and sensitivity rather than with evaluation and "maintaining standards", which the writer must meet or else. He and the writer represent rather, I thought, the theory and practice respectively of the same activity. That did not mean, and could never possibly mean, that the critic's function was to influence the poet or tell him how he should write or what he should write about. But I felt that poetry and criticism, *Dichtung* and *Wahrheit*, imaginative expression and conceptual expression, were linked on equal terms in a dialectical relationship none the less, whenever they appeared in the same culture.

It was clear that to follow up this conviction one would need to expand and redefine the conception of criticism. If I was right, what I said would be confirmed by the cultural developments taking place around me. Matthew Arnold, in his essay on "The Function of Criticism at the Present Time" and elsewhere, had spoken of the essential role of criticism in the maturing of a culture, from which the poet would directly benefit. But he also assumed that the critical faculty was "lower" than the creative one, and I felt that this Romantic baggage of high and low metaphors was getting to be a nuisance. Some of my colleagues, notably A.S.P. Woodhouse, were absorbed by a scholarly interest to which they gave the name "history of ideas." It seemed to me that these "ideas" were really elements or units in what Tillyard calls a world picture, the conceptual aspect of a kind of cosmology of imagery and metaphor that every poet who works on a large scale seems to work with, and that seems to preserve its main outlines for centuries, however much it may alter in detail from one age to another. Earlier poets could take such a world picture for granted, as something already formed by religious and political thought. In such passages as Ulysses' speech on degree in *Troilus and Cressida* we glimpse something of the framework of theoretical assumptions that Shakespeare depended on his audience's possessing. But these traditional frameworks had largely collapsed by the end of the eighteenth century, and new poetic structures would need new conceptual ones. Hence when Arnold spoke of "criticism", he meant partly what was traditionally meant by that word, but he was also speaking of something new, something just coming into being that had barely taken form in his day.

Reviewing, of which I did a good deal in the fifties, is a *hermeneutic* activity, which means that it is a form of writing in which understanding and the articulating of that understanding become the same thing. It is also a species of translation: the poet writes in a specific language of symbolism, myth, imagery and metaphor, and the reviewer renders that language in a different conceptual framework. Literature is one of the practical imaginative arts: criticism is one of the scholarly areas loosely called the humanities. It was clear that a great deal of shifting and regrouping of forces in the humanities was taking place. Toronto has always emphasized the importance of undergraduate teaching, and the undergraduate teaching of English literature is a very large activity, as it will be for the foreseeable future. But literary scholarship was beginning to resemble the well-known caterpillar, staring at a butterfly and saying "you'll never catch me going up in one of those things". As a student in the early thirties I had had to answer vague examination questions about a writer's "style"; as a teacher in the early forties I had to learn something quite specific about stylistics and rhetorical devices. No colleague or student of Woodhouse could avoid the challenge of the fact that history and philosophy were not just "background" for literature but were an essential part of literary criticism itself. Writers beyond the Toronto horizon at that time told me that anthropology and psychology were no less relevant.

The question then arose, what was this larger body of criticism of which literary criticism, as traditionally practised, seemed to be forming a smaller and smaller part? It was evidently something like "human science" of the kind adumbrated by Dilthey and others, but its total shape was still vague. The social scientists would have nothing to do with the suggestion that they were the applied humanities, nor did psychologists and anthropologists take much interest in the kind of use literary critics made of their material. I was aware of the rapid rise and influence of linguistics, especially synchronic linguistics, but, in striking contrast to the humane flexibility of nineteenth-century philology, linguistics was still a somewhat sectarian activity, not greatly interested even in literature, which it sometimes seemed almost to regard as a disease of language. But other movements were overriding this attitude, if I am right in thinking it existed. Gadamer, who is naturally thinking in a German context, says that the modern hermeneutic attitude, based on identifying *intelligere* and *explicare*, was established by the Romantic philosophers following Kant, and he adds that the effect of this was to move language from the periphery into the centre of the human sciences.

It was not until the mid-sixties, with the rise of European structuralism and the conception of the "linguistic model", that I began to see something of the shape of what was emerging, and to see also where such figures as Wittgenstein and Heidegger belonged in the pattern. I am not sure how deeply Canadian criticism even yet has been affected by these developments: Dennis Lee's *Savage Fields* is an example of a critical approach that one hopes will soon be less exceptional. But I did learn three things of relevance to this question while writing about Canadian culture. One came from the editorial committee that had gathered under Carl Klinck to plan the *Literary History of Canada*. It was obvious to all of us from the start that a history of what would conventionally be called Canadian literature would be an utterly pointless cream-skimming operation. The book had to be an exhaustive survey of *writing* in Canada, whatever the subject written about, if the real "literary" element in Canadian culture was to be captured. The second came from the fact that I was drawing support and suggestions and insights from such writers as George Grant, Abraham Rotstein, Carl Berger, Frank Underhill, who represented a great variety of academic "disciplines", but whose writing I could not think of as anything but Canadian "criticism". The third came from my personal knowledge of Canadian scholars, such as the authors of the books I saw at Harvard. I could not feel that their scholarship would have been exactly the same wherever they lived. I knew that my own interest in Blake had been sparked by the way he made imaginative sense out of the Nonconformist attitude that I had been brought up in myself. And whenever a Canadian scholar makes a personal statement, as, say, Kathleen Coburn does in her autobiography, *In Pursuit of Coleridge*, it becomes clear that scholarship, no less than poetry, grows out of a specific environment and is in part a response to it.

It is no great credit to me that I entirely missed the significance, at the time, of the later work of Harold Innis, which appeared around 1950-52. I found the prose style impenetrable and the subject matter uncongenial. But, of course, as is widely recognized now, Innis was defining a central issue in the Canadian imagination which ultimately affected the interests of practically everyone concerned with words. Innis had first, as an economist, studied the fur trade and the fishing industry, and had gained from that study a vision of the "Laurentian" centrifugal economic development of the country, with the traders and trappers fanning out from the Great Lakes into the far north. This in turn provided him with the underlying pattern of the primary modes of communication in Canada, the network of railways and canals mentioned above. After that, he asked himself the fateful question: "O.K., what happens next?" This took him into a panoramic vision of secondary communication through words, as conveyed by papyrus, paper, parchment, clay bricks, manuscripts, books and newspapers. He saw that verbal communication was an essential instrument of power, and that an ascendant class will naturally try to control and monopolize it. In *Empire and Communication*, and in the more accessible essays in *The Bias of Communication*, he sketched the outlines of a philosophy of history, based on the theme of the production and the control of the means of communication, on a scale as comprehensive, at least potentially, as anything since Marx. Like Marx, too, he left a large mass of *Grundrisse* to be published after his death.

Innis's influence, in Canada as elsewhere, will grow steadily, because with practice in reading him he becomes constantly more suggestive and rewarding. He was a curiously tentative writer, which may account for something of his rather spastic prose rhythm. He saw that every new form or technique generates both a positive impulse to exploit it and a negative impulse, especially strong in universities, to resist it, and that the former of course always outmanoeuvres the latter. But he had something of what I call the garrison mentality in him, the university being still his garrison for all the obscurantism in it that he comments on so dryly. Perhaps it is not possible to hold a vision of that scope and range steadily in one's mind without a more passionate commitment to society as well as to scholarship.

Marshall McLuhan, a literary critic interested originally in Elizabethan rhetoric and its expression in both oral and written forms, followed up other issues connected with the technology of communication, some of them leads from Innis. His relation to the public was the opposite of Innis's: he was caught up in the manic-depressive roller coaster of the news media, so that he was hysterically celebrated in the sixties and unreasonably neglected thereafter. It is likely that the theory of communications will be the aspect of the great critical pot-pourri of our time which will particularly interest Canadians, and to which they will make their most distinctive contribution. So it is perhaps time for a sympathetic rereading of *The Gutenberg Galaxy* and *Understanding Media* and a reabsorption of McLuhan's influence, though no adequate treatment of this topic can be attempted here.

I have often noted that many nineteenth-century writers in Canada, especially poets, spoke in what could be called, paraphrasing the title of Francis Sparshott's remarkable poem, the rhetoric of a divided voice. Up above was vigor and optimism and buoyancy and all the other qualities of life in a new land with lots of natural resources to exploit; underneath were lonely, bitter, brooding visions of cruelty without and despair within. This division in tone is still in Pratt, in a different way, and can even be traced in later writers, such as Layton, though the context naturally changes. It is by no means confined to Canada, as a reading of Whitman would soon show, but it is traditional here. McLuhan put a similar split rhetoric into an international context. On top was a breezy and self-assured butterslide theory of Western history, derived probably from a Chestertonian religious orientation, according to which medieval culture has preserved a balanced way of life that employed all the senses, depended on personal contact, and lived within "tribal", or small community units. Since then we have skittered down a slope into increasing specialization (McLuhan defines the specialist as the man who never makes a minor mistake on his way to a major fallacy), a self-hypnotism from concentrating on the visual stimuli of print and mathematics, a dividing and subdividing of life into separated "problems", and an obsession with linear advance also fostered by print and numbers. The electronic media, properly understood and manipulated, could reverse the direction of all this. Below was a horrifying vision of a global village, at once completely centralized and completely decentralized, with all its senses assailed at once, in a state of terror and anxiety at once stagnant and chaotic, equally a tyranny and an anarchy. His phrase "defence against media fallout" indicated this direction in his thought.

In the sixties both the anti-intellectuals, who wanted to hear that they had only to disregard books and watch television to get with it, and the "activists" pursuing terror for its own sake, found much to misunderstand in McLuhan. Many of his theses involved research in linguistics, anthropology, sensory psychology and economics which has still to be done or established even in those fields, and his recurring tendency to determinism involved him in prophecies not borne out by events. Media may be hot or cool, but societies do not turn hot or cool in consequence of adopting them. Canada is a cool country with cool people in it, hence all its media are cool. But McLuhan raised questions that are deeply involved in any survey of contemporary culture, and in any attempt to define the boundaries of the emerging theory of society that I call "criticism" in its larger context.

Meanwhile Canada's own involvement with new media, more particularly film and radio, had been a decisive influence in maturing the culture of the country and giving it a place in the international scene. I have no space or expertise to tell the story of the golden age of the NFB and CBC radio in the forties and early fifties. That has been done before, and it is generally recognized that film and radio are the media of much of the best work produced in Canadian culture. The benefits extended into literature, through radio plays and such programmes as *Anthology*, and Andrew Allan and Robert Weaver are names of the same kind of significance in Canadian writing that publishers like Briggs had in the nineteenth century. Radio also influenced, I think, the development of a more orally based poetry, more closely related to recitation and a listening audience, and popular in a way that poetry had not been for many centuries. As I write this, an anthology of "sound texts" comes in, poems based on sound and removed from ordinary syntax, and I notice that Canadian poets are deeply involved in this movement.

But there were difficulties that the coming of television made painfully obvious. These three new media, film, radio and television, are mass media, and consequently follow the centrifugal and imperial rhythms of politics and economics more readily than the regionalizing rhythms of culture. This was not too crucial a problem for CBC radio, though it was certainly there, but the NFB had to struggle with problems of distribution created by the fact that movie houses had been monopolized by American syndicates.

I remember a Spring Thaw skit which was a takeoff of an NFB film, ending with the line "on view in your local Sunday-School basement". So when television came the government passed a Broadcasting Act and set up the CRTC as a regulating agency for both radio and television, and both private and subsidized networks. I became an advisory member of the CRTC in 1968, when the Broadcasting Act still made a good deal of sense. The feeling was that the distribution of books, newspapers, movies and magazines had been very largely sold out to American interests, and that if television were the same way there would be no Canadian identity left.

For the next decade what seemed like a completely autonomous technological development started to explode: microwave, cable, satellite, and now a metamorphosis of pay-TV. It was not autonomous, of course, but Canadian identity, in that area, began to look as desperate as a Spartan at Thermopylae. Nor could a regulating agency even count on the support of public opinion: when Canada was, in the stock phrase, "flooded with American programmes," it was clear that the majority of Canadians preferred the flood to any Canadian ark that would float above it. Further, television is expensive to produce, and there have been many complaints that not only the CBC but the educational stations set up by the wealthier provinces have become mired in real estate, bureaucracy, and vested interests. Many viewers living in or near Toronto say that they cling to the PBS station in Buffalo, looking for a standard of programming from it that they no longer expect from Canadian sources, and some of them, noting the frequent PBS appeals for money, draw the inference that limited funds may be a stimulus of livelier thinking. The provinces are demanding a larger share of control of communications, but their motives for doing so are not cultural ones.

So a "mass culture" which follows expanding economic rather than regionalizing rhythms complicates the situation I have been outlining very considerably. Certainly there is much in it at present which is not Canadian in any sense and expresses very little creative energy. On the other hand all the mass media seem to have an entire cultural history to recapitulate, from the most archaic crudity to the greatest technical, and eventually creative, sophistication. There are still bad movies and dull radio programs, just as there are still bad books, but a listener to FM radio today or a moviegoer is a long way from the world of Amos and Andy or the Keystone Cops. Television is more frustrating and is still largely formulaic, but it too seems to be maturing in obedience to an inner process of development. I think the inherent tendency of television, as of film and radio, is to decrease the distinction between highbrow and lowbrow listeners, and within its widening central area of appeal to find more room for a greater variety of tastes.

In the sixties a resistance movement against the mass culture of (mainly) television grew up in the United States, and the magic word that explained everything that was then going on in this area was the word "sub-culture". But a sub-culture, whether its interest was in rock or drugs or meditation, showed a strong tendency to become mass news, featured on television networks or being reflected in fashion advertising. In other words these sub-cultures seemed to be really specialized forms of mass culture. Perhaps genuine culture is also the genuine form of sub-culture. No matter how complex the technical means of communication, the elements communicated are still words, tones, and images, the same elements that have been around since the earliest stone age. And I feel there is hope that the genuine article will continue, quietly but persistently and increasingly, to filter through the new technology.

National Consciousness in Canadian Culture

I was once present at a public hearing of the Canadian Radio and Television Commission, when leaders of the Cree Indian and Eskimo peoples in the far north were protesting against the destroying of their cultures by the mass media. One of them said that the overwhelming impression made on them by the media was that life in the south was "soft, violent, and sick". Some months later I was present at another CRTC hearing, on violence in television. There it was said that violence was an American phenomenon, being a cheap way of producing programmes for a huge mass market, and not a problem in Canada, except as a result of importing American programmes into Canada by cable. The conclusion of the second hearing was oddly similar to that of the first. There is no question of one group of people being inherently less violent than another: the principle involved is simply the elementary arithmetic of original sin. More people are always worse than fewer people.

At the same time more people are more aggressive and highly organized, and can force that organization on less populous communities. It seems doubtful at present that much of what is distinctive about the indigenous cultures of the north will long survive. One of their spokesmen asked us on the CRTC if we realized what an in-joke such a programme as *All in the Family* seemed in Frobisher or Aklavik. But probably, before long, that unpleasant family will become part of their family too. Similarly, our undefended border is very effectively defended on one side, the United States being a highly protectionist country in culture as in other aspects of life, and the Canadian instinct for compromise has to make the best of it. If a Canadian novelist writes about people in Manitoba and wishes to find an American publisher, it is relatively easy for him (or her: I am thinking particularly of the ill-starred career of Martha Ostenso) to push them over the border into North Dakota, in deference to the publisher's conviction that his readers will have a nervous breakdown if they pick up a novel with a Canadian setting. Some of Stephen Leacock's most unmistakably Canadian vignettes, in *Arcadian Adventures with the Idle Rich* and elsewhere, have American settings for the same reason. Again, if Canadian university graduates are excluded from the American job market and Canadian universities are full of Americans who make no concessions to their Canadian environment, it is easy for Canadians to rationalize the situation by saying that scholarship, like Canada, has no defended boundaries. Perhaps only intellectuals worry about cultural distinctiveness, and perhaps only because they have invented most of it themselves. The CRTC has constantly been reminded, first by broadcasters and later by cable operators, that the majority of Canadians prefer American programmes, including the brutal ones.

And yet this represents a temptation to be fought against. I detected a certain desperation in the statements of the Cree and Eskimo leaders, a feeling which was more than simply a fear that their cultures were being exterminated by the high-powered death-wish of southern civilization. It was rather a feeling that their own people might not care very much if they did lose their distinctive identity and simply merged into the Canadian mass. There would be strong economic arguments for their doing so, if not cultural ones. One hears the same tone among French-speaking Canadians, opposing the way that Canadian French so often breaks down into an English dialect, or the way that so many ambitious young Francophones accept English as their career language. One hears it among spokesmen for ethnical minorities, including Jewish leaders who seem almost to regret the decline of anti-Semitism, and of course among English-speaking

Canadians, where the threat to distinctiveness is regularly associated with America. But when we look at the United States itself, we can see that there is nothing American in the debasing of standards: that is simply human inertia, and such inertia destroys everything distinctive in American life equally with Canada.

The fight for cultural distinctiveness, from this point of view, is a fight for human dignity itself, for the variety in life that nothing but genuine culture can ever produce, for the unity that is at the opposite pole from uniformity. Many years ago Toynbee defined one of the central problems of society as the need to foster what he called creative minorities without allowing the emergence of what he called a dominant minority. Our current struggles for "affirmative action", our repudiation of "elitism", and the like, get this issue very confused at times, but it remains a genuine issue, especially when it is not recognized to be one, as is so often true of the United States vis-à-vis Canada. And to distinguish what is creative in a minority from what attempts to dominate, we have to distinguish between cultural issues, which are inherently decentralizing ones, and political and economic issues, which tend to centralization and hierarchy.

It is easy for those outside Canada to exaggerate the influence and persistence of the British connection on Canadian cultural development. It often comes as a surprise to my American friends that Canadians need passports to enter Great Britain, even though when they get there they go through a special door marked "Commonwealth". The British connection in Canada was culturally most important in the period between Confederation and the First World War. At that time Canada was trying to think of itself as a single nation extending "from sea to sea". As there was so much empty space in between, the Canadian consciousness could hardly match the American sense of a vast society slowly pushing a frontier westward until it reached the Pacific. Canada had to think of itself rather as part of a world-circling empire, its railways filling the gap in communication between Europe and the East, its natural resources contributing to a global technology, its young men taking part in the only social activity they were really wanted for outside Canada, imperial wars. As Charles G.D. Roberts says:

> And some Canadian lips are dumb
> Beneath Egyptian sands.

The American influence on Canadian literature in English has always been at least as direct and immediate as the British influence, and often more so. Cultural connections with Britain were of course close all through the nineteenth century, but they were no closer than those in the New England of Emerson and Henry James. In fact Canadians felt that there was far less attention paid to them in Great Britain than they would have got if they had come from a sovereign state. There is a story, recorded in Smollett's *Humphry Clinker*, of the delight of George II on being told that a rumor that the French had marched on Louisburg from Acadia must have been false, because Cape Breton is an island. This story symbolizes much in the British connexion that still rankles in the Canadian consciousness. I have elsewhere made the obvious but often overlooked observation that the French lost Canada mainly because they had very little interest in holding it, and that if they had held it they might well have sold it as they did Louisiana. The British took a less parochial view of their empire, but still their flaccid attitude to Canadian interests, from the Treaty of Ghent in 1814 through all the nineteenth-century boundary disputes, gave Canada a strong sense of not getting the support it needed for its unusually difficult problem of identity. Nobody has much use for a colony, apparently, or at least for the human part of it.

It is a standard practice of universities in settled areas, like Harvard or Yale or Toronto, to send its graduates out to civilize the boondocks and then recall them when they have become "established" scholars with nothing much more to say. This is the situation that looms large in the writings of Haliburton, early in the nineteenth century. For all his commitment to the colonial position, Haliburton felt that it developed laziness and over-dependence on the mother country, and he thought that his Yankee peddler Sam Slick was a model of what greater energy could do for Nova Scotia, however detached a view he took of Sam Slick's opinions and language. But the greatest energy would be useless unless it coincided with a more actively concerned response from Britain, and Haliburton felt that Britain should be much more active and discriminating in rewarding outstanding service in the colonies, beginning with him. Of the Church of England, for example, he makes Sam Slick say:

> Remove the restrictions on colonial clergy, so that if they desarve promotion in the church to Britain, they needn't be shut out among big bogs, black logs, and thick fogs, for ever and ever.

In other words, the colonies are essentially penal settlements, and should be regarded as, at least for the well-meaning and deserving, a purgatory rather than a hell.

Another passage in this same paper, from *The Attaché*, is even more striking. At the end of his life Haliburton went to Britain and entered politics there, joining the Conservative party because he thought it was conservative, though by his Bluenose standards of conservatism it was practically a Communist front. We may remember the book called *White Niggers of America*, a manifesto of radical French Canadian protest. It is interesting that identically the same metaphor had been used over a century earlier by the deeply conservative Haliburton to describe the English-speaking colonists in British North America:

> The slave is a slave, and that's his condition. Now the English have two sorts of niggers — American colonists, who are free white niggers; and manufacturers' laborers at home, and they are white slave niggers ... A colonist and a free nigger don't differ in anythin' but color: both have naked rights, but they have no power given 'em to clothe those rights, and that's the naked truth.

It seems to me better to think of Canada, not simply as British America, but as culturally descended from the Tory opposition to the Whig triumph at the time of the Revolutionary War. This is a view of it that would, *mutatis mutandis*, include French Canada, which still flies the pre-revolutionary flag of the lilies. The American assumption that freedom and national independence were inseparable never took as deep root in Canada, and the uninhabited American development of entrepreneur capitalism was hardly possible in a country equally large but so sparsely populated. Hence it was natural for Canada to combine Tory attitudes with radical ones, just as it was possible, in fact necessary, for it to achieve a fairly high degree of socialization. Most Canadian politicians, whatever their parties or personal beliefs, are compelled to be middle-of-the-road trimmers, for obvious reasons we do not need to go into. But many leading Canadian intellectuals, English or French, could be described as one form or other of Tory radical.

The distinctive is not the unique: what is distinctive is an emphasis, a special proportioning of elements that other societies may have in different proportions. I see something distinctive, in this sense, in the remark of R.H. Bonnycastle, writing in 1841, when he speaks of "the United States, where from the great mixture of races, British feelings and British connexion have given way before a flood of undefinable notions about liberty and equality, mixed with aristocratic wealth, slavery, and bigotry in religion". I am quoting this not for its insight but for its commonplaceness. What the writer dislikes is not only American democracy but American oligarchy, the inequalities of wealth and opportunity. The criticism attacks from both sides of the Whig establishment. In the literature of social protest in Canada we find, over and over, a kind of radicalism that seems closer to Tom Paine than to Jefferson, often because, like Paine, it has immediate British roots.

Similarly in Susanna Moodie's *Roughing it in the Bush* (1852), the positive virtues of what I have elsewhere called a garrison society show up with great clarity: the constant fight to be clean, fully clothed, disciplined in speech and manner, to maintain any number of standards that we may think unnecessary even though now they would be easy to maintain, emerges with a singular intensity of dedication. Susanna Moodie's effort to remain a gentlewoman in the backwoods makes her the exact opposite of what Carlyle means by an unworking aristocracy. She felt that she belonged to the gentry, and devoted all her waking moments to dramatizing her social status. But to do so she was often forced to accept conditions of life that were primitive to the point of squalor. It is no good saying that she had servants to help her put on her show: servants were the most disheartening of all her problems.

A culture founded on a revolutionary tradition, like that of the United States, is bound to show very different assumptions and imaginative patterns from those of a culture that rejects or distrusts revolution. First, an underlying assumption of a successful revolution is "violence pays", and the violence in American life, through the opening of the West to the gangsterism in the immense cities, is part of its revolutionary heritage. In Canada, developing as it did through a series of military occupations, where the red-coated "Mountie", half-policeman and half soldier, has become a national symbol, the violence has been mainly repressive violence. This means that nine-tenths of it never gets beyond the individual himself, or at most his immediate family. For details of how this self-destructive violence operates, see Canadian fiction, more or less passim: Margaret Atwood's lively book, *Survival*, is written largely about these indecisive "victor-victim" conflicts in Canadian novels. Such a mood, so largely disseminated through society, does not always make for colourful history. Dennis Lee, in his *Civil Elegies*, studies the curious paralysis of the 1837 rebellion, which took the form of

the first
spontaneous mutual retreat in the history of warfare

because the rebels did not believe in the logic of rebellion, and their opponents did not believe in the logic of repression. And today, when not only Quebec but Western and Eastern Canada have strong separatist sentiments, separatism is neutralized by a feeling, affecting separatists and federalists alike, that the issue is not really important enough to go beyond the stage of symbolism. Even symbolism has had a curiously muted life in Canada. Older cultural nationalists, for example, warned us against the dangers of "flag-waving", disregarding the fact that Canada at the time had no flag to wave. A Newfoundlander told me once that he thought his people had most in common with the Poles, and like them tended to celebrate defeats rather than victories. This was some years before the publication of Ray Smith's story, "Cape Breton is the Thought Control Centre of Canada", which makes the same point for Canada generally. Certainly Canada has been quite as persistently partitioned throughout most of its history: the penalty it pays for having natural resources.

Then again, a revolutionary tradition is a deductive one: it implies a written constitution, which has to be reinterpreted or amended as time goes on, with major premises about human rights, the sense of a break with the past and of continuity with the future. The United States was fortunate in achieving this articulating process in the eighteenth century, perhaps the only time in Western history when reason looked reasonable. The contemporary Quebec Act was the opposite of all this: it consolidated the past, recognized the *de facto* equality of two groups of people divided by language, legal tradition, and very largely by religion,

and made an *ad hoc* settlement on the basis later developed
theoretically by Burke, of resolving a conflict by recognizing some
of the interests on both sides. It provided no blueprint for an
indefinite future: it merely solved one crisis with some hope that it
would last until the next one. The two countries, with their
national birthdays only two days apart, were born under much the
same stars, but have reacted to them very differently. In the United
States there has been, until recently, a sense of progressive and
linear advance, a progress like that of an express train into a future
logically related to the past. Everyone quotes the penultimate
sentence in *Huckleberry Finn* about lighting out for the Territory,
but less attention is paid to the even more significant last sentence:
"I been there before". There can be no creative return to the past:
the past is absorbed into the future, or, as Whitman says:

> As a projectile form'd, impell'd, passing a certain line,
>   still keeps on,
> So the present, utterly form'd, impell'd by the past.

This sense of progress derives from a society which has
defined its aims and is aware of its assumptions, and the individual
defines himself against that society, usually as some kind of
explorer or pioneer, whether the frontier implied is physical or
cultural. Canada never defined itself as a unified society in this
way: there is no Canadian way of life, no hundred per cent
Canadian, no ancestral figures corresponding to Washington or
Franklin or Jefferson, no eighteenth-century self-evident certain-
ties about human rights, no symmetrically laid out country.
Washington became a capital because it was in the logical place
for one, between the north and the south: Ottawa became a capital
because it was not Montreal or Kingston. A sardonic com-
mentator, writing in 1868, remarks that its name was obviously
derived from "Hoot awa", or out of the way. The Canadian sense
of the future tends to be apocalyptic: Laurier's dictum that the
twentieth century would belong to Canada was, even then,
implying a most improbable and discontinuous future. The past
in Canada, on the other hand, is, like the past of a psychiatric
patient, something of a problem to be resolved: it is rather like
what the past would be in the United States if it had started with
the Civil War instead of the Revolutionary War.

American culture has followed the Western pattern, which
grew out of the Biblical rejection of what it called "idolatry", that

is, the belief that there was something numinous or potentially divine in the natural world. For the Western tradition, man must seek his God or his ideals through his social institutions. Nature is not to be worshipped or even loved: it is to be dominated. Canada tried hard to follow the same pattern, but its society has been less cohesive, and the individual poet or painter finds that it keeps disintegrating: it is hard for him to visualize either the audience in front of him that he is trying to reach or the audience behind him out of which his imagination has grown. In this situation the natural world keeps pushing insistently through the gaps in the mental society. I see constantly in Canadian culture, more particularly in its poetry, a sense of meditative shock produced by the intrusion of the natural world into the imagination. I say intrusion, because it so often looms up with a greater urgency than the poet's social, political or religious outlook is prepared to allow for.

I imagine that W.L. Morton is right in connecting this sense in Canada with the role of the northern frontier in the Canadian imagination. An American who had never seen the Mississippi would not be regarded as a widely travelled man, at least in his own country; but few Canadians have ever seen the largest river in Canada, the Mackenzie, and the existence of a vast hinterland which is both a part of us and yet not a part of us creates something curiously self-alienating. Morton says:

> And because of this separate origin in the northern frontier, economy, and approach, Canadian life to this day is marked by a northern quality, the strong seasonal rhythm which still governs even academic sessions . . . The line which marks off the frontier from the farmstead, the wilderness from the baseland, the hinterland from the metropolis, runs through every Canadian psyche.

The last sentence might be equally true of the psyches in Colorado or Arkansas or Oregon: what is different is that in the United States wilderness and baseland can be assimiliated by a uniting consciousness. In Canada the wilderness, symbolized by the north, creates a kind of doppelganger figure who is oneself and yet the opposite of oneself. I remember being at a "church supper" in a rural area of Saskatchewan, and hearing one woman say to another: "you know, this last rain wasn't necessary, in the least". It nearly split my own Canadian psyche to hear, in so middle-class a gathering, the murmur of a timeless peasantry scolding its household gods. But such sudden atavisms are almost a commonplace in Canadian literature, whether the setting is rural or urban.

I have often spoken of the presbyopic sense in Canadian culture, the vast distances of river and sky that confer nobility on faraway looks. Donald Creighton, a great master of Canadian rhetoric, ends the first volume of his biography of John A. MacDonald with this sentence:

> They [the parliament buildings] stood out boldly against the sky; and far behind them, hidden in darkness, were the ridges of the Laurentians, stretching away, mile after mile, towards the north-west.

The last sentence of the second volume reads:

> Beyond the dock lay the harbour and the islands which marked the end of the lowest of the Great Lakes; and beyond the islands the St. Lawrence River began its long journey to the sea.

I have previously noted the same perspective in Canadian painters, notably in Tom Thomson's canoeist's eye that is continually scanning the horizon for some break into still greater distance. The tree in the centre of Thomson's "West Wind" seems deliberately out of visual focus: the eye is led to something behind it. Yet it seems also to be saying: "Look, I belong here: I'm not just an obstacle on the way to the horizon". It is an emblem of Canada itself, so long apologetic for being so big an obstacle on the way to somewhere more interesting, yet slowly becoming a visible object in its own right.

At the very beginning of Canadian literature in English, we have Frances Brooke's *The History of Emily Montague* (1769), in which the narrator remarks:

> Nothing is, in my opinion, so favourable to the display of beauty as a ball. A state of rest is ungraceful . . . never any human being had such an aversion to still life as I have.

A very innocent and light-hearted remark; but a great deal of Canadian cultural history is summed up in it: the obsession with movement and transportation, the eye that passes over the foreground object, the restlessness that solves all social difficulties by moving somewhere else, the commitment to a society that involves constant movement up and down an immensely long and narrow corridor. Two centuries later than Emily's proclamation of her aversion to still life, E.J. Pratt wrote a poem called "Still Life" which uses that phrase as a term of contempt for poets who do not deal with the great moving issues of society. It is the only poem of his I know with a real tone of hostility in it. Still later we have Gwendolyn MacEwen, in a poem called "The Portage", commenting on the same feature in the Canadian sensibility:

> But now we fear movement
> and now we dread stillness;
> we suspect it was the land
> that always moved, not our ships . . .

I spoke of Susanna Moodie and her struggle to maintain the social perspective to which she had become accustomed in the unrelenting surroundings of the Canadian bush. Her sister Catharine Parr Traill is, at least superficially, a more attractive personality, making the best of her hardships and cultivating an interest in the nature around her that makes her a kind of miniature Thoreau, especially in her studies of flowers. She says: "To the person who is capable of looking abroad into the beauties of nature, and adoring the Creator through his glorious works, are opened stores of unmixed pleasure, which will not permit her to be dull or unhappy in the loneliest part of our Western Wilderness". The word "her" is worth pausing on for a moment: it seems to be assumed that a woman's life, however arduous the conditions, will show a relatively civilized balance between work and leisure, whereas the male, whether hunter or fisherman or farmer, will merely oscillate between work and idleness. As an early (1818) writer in Newfoundland remarks: "all ranks of society appear to consider debauchery as the only antidote to the *taedium vitae* which prevails between the month of December and the recommencement of the fishery in the May following". Perhaps we have a clue here to the large proportion of women among the best Canadian writers. Mrs. Traill's capacity for detailed attention to "still life" is exceptional, if not unique, in early Canadian writing: at the same time she sometimes gives the impression of having too fixed a smile, too determined a cheerfulness, too resolute to exclude many things she doesn't want yet knows to be there. One suspects that the two qualities are psychologically close together.

What I mean by a meditative shock produced by the natural world in Canadian poetry is not easy to explain, but some

examples may clarify it. Let us first take a passage in Isabella
Valancy Crawford's *Malcolm's Katie* (1884) that rather upset E.K.
Brown, in his pioneering study of Canadian poetry:

> And Max car'd little for the blotted sun,
> And nothing for the startl'd, outshone stars;
> For Love, once set within a lover's breast,
> Has its own Sun — its own peculiar sky,
> All one great daffodil — on which do lie
> The sun, the moon, the stars — all seen at once . . .

The metamorphosis of distant nature into a single "great
daffodil" inside the mind is a kind of imaginative explosion, in
which the overlooked and peripheral suddenly turns into something overmastering and central. Or take Frederick Philip Grove's
description of a July storm on the prairies in *The Turn of the Year*.
There is a flash of lightning followed by thunder, as there so often
is in thunderstorms: nothing really happens, and a minute later a
"little girl comes out, barefooted, to splash in the pools". What is
left in the narrator's mind is very curious:

> Like a desert of barren snow is my mind, a white blank, stunned
> into unconsciousness of all things about me. But like a scarlet
> patch of blood shed on a real snowfield there lies on the white
> impassive background of my vision the memory of that frightful
> clap of wrath.

The image has nothing clearly to do with summer storms: it is the
central image of Canadian fear and guilt: the blank world of white
snow stained with the blood of murdered animals. In Irving
Layton's "A Tall Man Executes a Jig", a man watches a wounded
grass snake "that lugged / Its intestine like a small red valise". It
finally dies, and there follows an extraordinary conclusion:

> Meanwhile the green snake crept upon the sky,
> Huge, his mailed coat glittering with stars that made
> The night bright, and blowing thin wreaths of cloud
> Athwart the moon; and as the weary man
> Stood up, coiled above his head, transforming all.

A poem of James Reaney, "The Heart and the Sun", describes a
love affair in which the heart swallows the sun but then dies, the
sun escaping with the final remark:

"Alas, my Love, it is your fate and mine
That I someday smother whom I kindle
And give birth to those I'll someday kill."

In these passages something casual and expected in nature goes through a vortex or gyre into the mind, and creates there a riddle of experience which cannot be assimilated to any set of human or social values. Like the gods of polytheism, it is neither good nor evil, but may be either or both. It is usually an object of involuntary contemplation, something that the mind has not consciously attended to but has forced its way in anyhow. It looks almost as though the fear of still life in the Canadian imagination were a fear of, so to speak, catching Nature's eye, as seen not merely in the eye of a dying animal but in the autumnal blaze of a dying leaf, or even, in Pratt's *Towards the Last Spike*, in the glitter of metals blasted by dynamite out of the pre-Cambrian shield.

The unbroken violation of nature in Canada, the economy founded on the trapping and mutilating of animals, the destroying of trees, the drying up of rivers and the polluting of lakes, began inspiring guilt and uneasiness long before the contemporary ecology movement. In Canadian poetry there is a special pathos in dying animals and falling trees, and in many tragic narratives, such as Duncan Campbell Scott's "At the Cedars" and Birney's *David*, where people are killed in log jams or on glaciers, there is a lurking sense not only of the indifference of nature to man, but almost of its exasperation with this parasite of humanity that has settled on it. In one of Ernest Thompson Seton's stories, a hunter is obsessed with the desire to kill a great mountain ram, simply because it is the most beautiful thing he has ever seen. He finally shoots it; reaction sets in; he cuts the head off and puts it on the wall of his cabin with a curtain over it and sits down to wait for the ram, as he says, to get even. Eventually a landslide buries him and his cabin. Modern ecology-conscious writing like that of Farley Mowat merely puts this conception of the nemesis of nature on a less fanciful basis.

We may also notice how often contemporary poets take the traditional Canadian theme of the identity of the hunter and the hunted, and turn it into the theme of metamorphosis, where the victorious human actually becomes the defeated animal, as in the story of Actaeon. We find this in Margaret Atwood's book of verse, *You Are Happy*, especially in the sequence called "Songs of the

Transformed", and the series of "Circe/Mud" poems which follows it. It is also prominent in Gwendolyn MacEwen's *Magic Animals*, in Susan Musgrave's Haida poems, and in the many poems about the descent to the darker levels of one's own consciousness, as in Jay Macpherson's *Welcoming Disaster* and Eli Mandel's Minotaur poems. Every so often this theme manifests the split within the psyche that Morton mentions. The poet becomes both a daylight consciousness and a dark shadow of that consciousness which identifies, very often, with a continuously martyred nature. In Francis Sparshott's remarkable long poem, *Rhetoric for a Divided Voice*, we have a dialogue between two halves of the same person, one questioning, the other more elusive and yet more certain of its knowledge. The part called "Half" says:

> I challenge your world to atone
> For my unmerited pain

and the "Other Half" answers:

> Breath is the wraith of frost,
> And breath drawn into hold
> In the temple of the ghost
> The marriage of dark and cold.
> Deep over hands and head
> Welcoming snow is thrown;
> Deep over head and hands
> To the levelling of broken lands,
> To the burial of the dead.

It is perhaps worth noticing that the best piece of science fiction in Canadian literature, James de Mille's *A Strange Manuscript Found in a Copper Cylinder*, not published until 1888 but written much earlier, describes a society dedicated to the opposite of all normal human ideals, to darkness, death, poverty and pain.

One could go on with many other examples, but these should make the point. The Tory opposition to the American way of life, which spoke as often from the left of it as from the right, was a strangled and muted voice as long as the United States was progressing, like Whitman's projectile, in more or less a straight line. Now the United States seems to be entering a period of self-examination, of taking a more retrospective look at its past and its traditional assumptions. It is even possible that American development has reached a climax and will see its past and future as more of a parabola. There are, of course, many movements of imaginative opposition within American literature itself paralleling the Canadian one. But simultaneously with the growth of a new feeling in the United States, there has been in English-speaking Canada, since about 1960, a great upsurge of creative power, both within the conventional forms of poetry and fiction and outside them. In French Canada the parallel upsurge, though equally remarkable, has taken more explicitly political forms. The Canadian recurring themes of self-conflict, of the violating of nature, of individuals uncertain of their social context, of dark, repressed, oracular doubles concealed within each of us, are now more communicable outside Canada in the new mood of the world. The assumption that exploiting nature is the only way to human advancement has lost much of its authority, and so has the geometry, reflected in the grid patterns of our cities and the like, that has ordered so much of our lives since the eighteenth century. Around 1900 the word "square" was a general term of approval: today it means something we are trying to get away from. I imagine that in another ten years there will be very little difference in tone between Canadian and American literature; but what there is now in Canada is a literature of extraordinary vigor and historical significance.

Sharing the Continent

Practically all Canadians have friends or relatives in the United States, and have spent a good deal of time there. Hence it is generally assumed, in both countries, that English-speaking Canadians, at least, cannot be told apart from Americans. This was a view that I held myself until I spent a couple of years in England as a student. Then I realized that there was a difference, but I found it hard to put the difference into words, and because our civilization is tied up in words, we are apt to think that whatever we can't verbalize is unreal. After that, I began an academic career, and have taught briefly at several American universities. My American students often ask me if I notice much difference between teaching them and teaching Canadians in Toronto. They usually expect the answer to be no, but my answer is yes. Here is, perhaps, something that it is possible to put into words. American students have been conditioned from infancy to think of themselves as citizens of one of the world's great powers. Canadians are conditioned from infancy to think of themselves as citizens of a country of uncertain identity, a confusing past, and a hazardous future. Nine-tenths of the time the responses of my American students are identical with those of Canadian students, but the tenth time I know that I'm in a foreign country and have no idea what the next move is. The sensation must be rather similar to that of a Dane in Germany or a Finn in Russia; or, on a smaller scale, of a Welshman in England. What I should like to try to do here is to define the areas of likeness and of difference a little more precisely. The history and the geography of the two countries have been so different that the cultural response to them has to be different too.

I begin with the geographical differences. Some years ago I first saw Herbert's Marcuse's *One-Dimensional Man* in a bookshop, and what came into my mind was a quite irrelevant reflection: "I wonder what he'd say if he had to live in a one-dimensional country?" For Canada, through most of its history, has been a strip of territory as narrow as Chile, besides being longer and more broken up. In the United States, the general historical pattern has been based on a north-south axis with a western frontier that moved gradually across mountains and rivers and prairies to the Pacific. In Canada there is a single gigantic east-west thrust down the St. Lawrence, up the Great Lakes, and across the prairies, then through whatever holes a surveyor could find in the Rockies to the west coast. Consider the emotional difference between coming to the United States by ship from England and coming to Canada. The United States presents a fairly symmetrical coastline, with relatively few islands, apart from a minor group in the mouth of the Hudson, and one is reminded of the old remark about Columbus' discovering America; "How could he have missed it?" One enters Canada through the Strait of Belle Isle into the Gulf of St. Lawrence, where five Canadian provinces surround us, with enormous islands and glimpses of a mysterious mainland in the distance, but in the foreground only sea and sky. Then we go down the waterway of the St. Lawrence, which in itself is only the end of a chain of rivers and lakes that starts in the Rockies. The United States confronts the European visitor; Canada surrounds and engulfs him, or did until the coming of the airplane.

In the United States, the frontier has been, imaginatively, an open-ended horizon in the west; in Canada, wherever one is, the frontier is a circumference. Every part of Canada is shut off by its geography, British Columbia from the prairies by the Rockies, the prairies from the Canadas by the immense hinterland of northern

Ontario, Quebec from the Maritimes by the upthrust of Maine, the Maritimes from Newfoundland by the sea. A generation ago, Hugh MacLennan took a phrase from Rilke, "two solitudes", as the title for a novel about the mutual isolation of English and French in Montreal. But everywhere in Canada we find solitudes touching other solitudes: every part of Canada has strong separatist feelings, because every part of it is in fact a separation. And behind all these separations lies the silent north, full of vast rivers, lakes and islands that, even yet, very few Canadians have ever seen. The Mississippi, running north to south through the middle of the country, is a symbol of the American frontier and its steady advance into the sunset. The largest river in Canada, the Mackenzie, pouring slightly into the Arctic Ocean at what seems the end of the earth, is a symbol of the *terra incognita* in Canadian consciousness, or what Rupert Brooke called the "unseizable virginity" of the Canadian landscape. Or, as another British visitor, Wyndham Lewis, remarked: "this monstrous, empty habitat must continue to dominate this nation psychologically, and so culturally".

In looking at two countries as closely related as Canada and the United States, no difference is unique or exclusive: we can point to nothing in Canada that does not have a counterpart, or many counterparts, south of its border. What is different is a matter of emphasis and of degree. In the United States, exploration and the building of railways have naturally been of central importance in the imagination of the country. In Canada they have been obsessive. The Confederation of 1867 depended on the building of a railway from one ocean to the other: the political necessity to keep the CPR entirely within Canada meant that the railway had to be built in the face of almost unimaginable natural obstacles. The CPR remained a private corporation, but the great difficulty of establishing communication in Canada meant that Canada became accustomed very soon to nationalized railways, broadcasting corporations, film boards, air lines, and similar efforts of deficit financing. Canadian culture has reflected the same preoccupations. The first wave of exploration was mainly religious and economic, carried on by missionaries and *voyageurs* and fur-traders, along with the explorers who worked in their interests. The second wave was technological and scientific, an age of railway building and geological surveys. The third wave was cultural, and was spearheaded by painters, from the earliest travelling and military artists of the nineteenth century, Krieghoff, Paul Kane, Thomas Davies, to the Group of Seven and their contemporaries a generation ago.

A strong documentary interest in painting, in films, even in literature, is an obvious and distinctive feature of Canadian culture, and it follows the tradition of the early explorers and missionaries, of the Jesuit Relations and the reports of the Hudson's Bay Company. But it is painting in particular that expresses this interest: painting, the art that began in the deep caves of paleolithic times, has always had something of an unborn world about it, the projecting on nature of colours in the dark, this last phrase being the title of a Canadian play by James Reaney. Painting is in the front line of imaginative efforts to humanize a non-human world, to fight back, in a sparsely-settled country, against a silent otherness that refuses to assimilate to anything human.

A fascination with landscape is the dominant feature of Canadian painting down to about 1930. Even in later and more abstract painters, Riopelle, for example, it seems to me that there is a strong basis of landscape in the underlying vision. The exploring and pioneering aspect of this is clearest in Tom Thomson, Emily Carr, and the Group of Seven, where we are still very largely in the Canada of the blazed trail and the canoe. The painter keeps shifting our eye from the foreground into the opening in the woods, the bend of the river, the break through the distant hills. The use of expressionist and fauve techniques, with powerful color-contrasts exploding against one another, suggests a natural world that is unconscious of man and is absorbed in an internecine battle of titans. In historical perspective another element emerges which is much more sinister than simply the unblinking stare of a stark "solemn land", as J.E.H. MacDonald called one of his best known paintings. Just as, in a crowded country like Great Britain, the practice of archaeology is a matter of keeping one jump ahead of the bulldozer, so these precious records of nature in her "unspoiled" loveliness of snow and rock and red sumach and maple seem to be hastily jotted notes of a hunted refugee, set down before civilization arrives and turns the scene into one more garbage dump.

Literature during this period did not fare so well as painting, because this long-range perspective in literature is very apt to turn rhetorical, in a rather bad sense. Thus Charles G.D. Roberts:

> Awake, my country, the hour is great with change!
>   Under this gloom which yet obscures the land,
> From ice-blue strait and stern Laurentian range
>   To where giant peaks our western bounds command,
> A deep voice stirs . . .
>   ("An Ode for the Canadian Confederacy").

I quote this because it is typical of what made so much Canadian poetry of a century ago immature and colonial. The poet is not expressing his feelings but talking about the feelings he thinks he ought to have, and the clue to his poetic insincerity is the remote surveying vision that is really focussed on nothing but a map. In other contexts this kind of rhetoric turns didactic, as in Bliss Carman's rather forced praises of the strenuous life. No poets of this period gave us the sense of an inward struggling nature that Thomson and Emily Carr do, except for some brilliant flashes in one writer, Isabella Crawford, who died unknown at 37. English-Canadian poetry had to wait for E.J. Pratt to convey the real sense of this centrifugal and linear rhythm in Canadian life. His themes are those that are most closely connected with this rhythm: the martyrdom of the Jesuit missionaries, the building of the CPR, the stories of whale hunts and shipwrecks that bring out the sense of a beleaguered and surrounded garrison.

I have been speaking of one direction in the Canadian imagination: the direction that followed the east-west Laurentian movement and responded emotionally to the national motto *a mari usque ad mare*. This was both a romantic and a conservative movement: romantic because it sought the new and the unknown, conservative because its original impetus was in Europe. The Confederation that took shape around a transcontinental railway was part of a global chain of communication that started in London and linked together all the pieces of an empire on which the sun never set. But as settlement in the country advanced, a more longitudinal and north-south consciousness developed. This perspective focussed on the American connection rather than the British Empire, and tended to see the country as a series of northern spurs of the United States. When I was growing up in the Maritime Provinces during the nineteen-twenties, there was a strong political loyalty to Confederation, but an even stronger sense that Boston was our real capital, and that the Maritimes formed the periphery of New England, or what was often called "the Boston states". In the nineteenth century, at least, the Liberal party reflected the north-south North American outlook, as the Conservative party reflected the Laurentian one.

Once again it is painting that gives us the clearest sense of the contrast. If we turn from the Group of Seven to the Quebec landscape painters, to Maurice Cullen, Suzor-Côté, Clarence Gagnon and the very little of Morrice that was done in Canada, we are in a world of softer and gentler outlines where the sense of being lived in shows through. The painter's eye is more restricted and at the same time more precise. The landscape is receding from a human eye, not absorbed in itself. Quebec is the only part of Canada which has been settled long enough for a sense of imaginative digestion, so to speak, to emerge. When E.J. Pratt spoke of a kind of poetry he disapproved of, a poetry that avoided social issues and cultivated an easy self-indulgence, he described it in the pictorial metaphor of "still life". In his use of this phrase there is, perhaps, something of that odd fear of catching nature's eye that is very characteristic of that stage in Canadian development. It is significant, first, that the best still-life painter in the earlier period, Ozias Leduc, lived and died in Quebec, and, second, that the still-life perspective, where the imagination has completely surrounded the subject, begins to emerge rather later than the Group of Seven, with David Milne, and further west, Lemoine Fitzgerald.

What has been gradually revealed in this development is the fact that cultural movements are different in direction and rhythm from political and economic ones. Politically and economically, the current of history is toward greater unity, and unity in this context includes uniformity. Technology is the most dramatic aspect of this development: one cannot take off in a jet plane and expect a radically different way of life in the place where the plane lands. But culture has something vegetable about it, something that increasingly needs to grow from roots, something that demands a small region and a restricted locale. The fifty states of the Union are not, in themselves, a cultural entity: they are a political and economic entity that provides a social background for a great variety of cultural developments. We speak for convenience of American literature, but its real cultural context usually turns out to be something more like Mississippi or New England or Chicago or an expatriate group in Paris. Even in the much smaller Great Britain we have Thomas Hardy largely confined to "Wessex", Dylan Thomas to South Wales, D.H. Lawrence to the Midlands. Similarly in Canada: as the country has matured, more and more of its local areas have come to life imaginatively.

This fact has given French Canadian writers, in particular, one considerable advantage. The French Canadian poet or novelist knows that he is contributing to the articulateness of a beleaguered language, hence he need have no doubt about his social function or the importance of being a writer in such a situation. He has no competitors closer than European France, and they live in a very different social context. The English Canadian writer has not had this advantage, and the tedium of a permanent identity crisis has afflicted English Canada for a century. Soon after the Second World War, French Canada entered what has been called the quiet revolution, an awareness of belonging both to itself and to the modern world, which shook off most of the isolating features that had been previously restricting its cultural life. I think it was partly a response to the French act of self-definition that made for a sudden and dramatic emergence of English Canadian culture after about 1960. Since then there has been a tremendous cultural explosion, in literature and painting particularly, which has produced a mood that is often called cultural nationalism.

This is a most misleading phrase, and for two reasons. First, nationalism suggests something aggressive, like a nineteenth-century jingoist waiting for the next war to start, or a twentieth-century third-world revolutionary. But culture in itself seeks only its own identity, not an enemy: hostility only confuses it. Second, contemporary Canadian culture, being a culture, is not a national development but a series of regional ones, what is happening in British Columbia being very different from what is happening in New Brunswick or Ontario. Even there we find an increasing decentralization: one reason why Montreal has been so lively a cultural centre is that there are a good many Montreals, each one with its own complexities and inner conflicts. Then again, while a certain amount of protection may be needed for Canadian writers and artists, cultural products are export products. If we look at, say, the literature that has come out of Ireland during the last century, we can see that culture, like a grain or wine crop, is produced in a local area but is not necessarily consumed there.

Politically, economically and technologically, the world is uniting; Canada is in the American orbit and will remain so for the foreseeable future. Canadians could not resist that even if they wanted to, and not many of them do want to. Culturally, both nations should run their own show, and the way to run a cultural show is to let a thousand flowers bloom, in Mao's phrase. Things go wrong when cultural developments are hitched on to economic or technological ones. That gives us, on this continent, a sub-culture dominated by advertising and distributed through the mass media. The influence of this in our lives is often spoken of, both inside and outside the United States, as an Americanizing influence. Ten years ago, during the centenary of Confederation, a sour little joke was circulating in Canada to the effect that what had been aimed at in Canada was a combination of British political institutions, American economic buoyancy and French culture, and that what we had, after a century, was French politics, British economic buoyancy, and American culture. However, the growth of an anonymous, mass-produced, mindless sub-culture is American only to the extent that the United States is the world's most highly industrialized society. Its effect on genuine American culture is quite as lethal as its effect everywhere else, and its main features are as Japanese or German or Russian as they are American.

Things go wrong in the opposite direction when economic or political developments are hitched on to cultural ones, as has happened in the Quebec separatist movement. It is a part of M. Levesque's sales pitch to speak of separation as inevitable, and to compare it with the American Revolution. It seems to me a retrograde and counter-historical movement, both in its neo-colonial attitude to France and in its arrogant attitude to French Canadians outside Quebec. As for the American analogy, what was of permanent importance there was not the separation from Britain but the principle of *e pluribus unum*: politically and economically, the colonies had to unite, though culturally there was no reason why Massachusetts and Virginia should not be quite different. Separatism in Quebec is an intellectuals' movement, a *trahison des clercs*: it has dominated the communications media for some years, and by-passes economic issues with a simple emotional construct in which Confederation equals bondage and separation freedom. As an intellectuals' movement, even a revolutionary one, it may settle for a purely symbolic separation: if it goes beyond that, whatever is distinctive in the culture of Quebec will be its first casualty.

My reasons for thinking so take me into the second group of conditioning differences from the United States, the historical ones. The pattern of Canadian history has been almost the opposite of the pattern of American history. The United States had a War of Independence against a European power in the eighteenth century, and a civil war on its own soil a century later. Canada had a civil war of European powers on its own soil in the eighteenth century, and a movement of independence against its American partner in the nineteenth. This started with the invasion of 1775 and continued in the war of 1812, which had very little point as a war with Britain, but was in many respects a war of independence for Canada. I discover that Americans, while they know about the bombardment of Washington and the battle of New Orleans, are often hardly aware that this war involved Canada at all, much less that the bombardment of Washington was a reprisal for the burning of what is now Toronto. All through the nineteenth century, up to and beyond Confederation, there continued to be a certain edginess about the aggressive expansion of America, as it came through in Fenian raids and boundary disputes, and Confederation itself completed what the American invasions had begun, the sense that there was an identity on the north side of the border that could be brought into being only by some kind of political unity.

Another historical contrast is even more important. The United States reached its peak of articulateness in the latter part of the eighteenth century, the age when it became a nation, the age of Washington, Adams, Jefferson, and Franklin. The United States is today the oldest country in the world: that is, no other nation has lasted so long with so relatively little social change. The party now in power is the world's oldest political party, and the American flag is one of the world's oldest flags. Canada, by contrast, had no eighteenth century. It started with the expansion of French Canada in the seventeenth century, and started again with the influx of defeated Tories into Ontario and the Maritimes after the

Revolution, going directly from Baroque to Romantic expansion, but never achieving the moment of self-definition that the United States achieved.

It would be a great mistake to exaggerate the strength of the British connexion in Canada, even in the nineteenth century. There was a great deal of superficial loyalty, or at least a good many expressions of it, but there was also much resentment, and a feeling that colonials would have been treated with more respect in London if, like Americans, they had represented an independent nation. Some years ago a book appeared in Quebec called *White Niggers of America*, meaning the French Canadians, an expression of strong separatist feelings in Quebec; but the same metaphor had been used over a century earlier by the deeply conservative Haliburton of Nova Scotia, who makes his Sam Slick remark that a colonial and a freed black slave differed in nothing but colour: they had theoretical rights but no power to enforce them.

It would, I think, make for a clearer sense of Canada if we thought of it, not as British North America, but as a country that grew out of a Tory opposition to the Whig victory in the American Revolution, thus forming, in a sense, something complementary to the United States itself. This may sound like a very English-based view of Canadian history, but I am not sure that it is. Not long after the British conquest came the French Revolution with its strongly anti-clerical bias. The clergy remained the ideologically dominant group in Quebec down to a generation ago, and the clergy wanted no part of the French Revolution or anything it stood for. Quebec still flies the pre-revolutionary flag of lilies. Nor, from that clergy's point of view, was the American Revolution really so different from the French one. But apart from the clerical influence, French Canada had excellent and foresighted reasons for accepting a conservative *modus vivendi* which, from the Quebec Act in the eighteenth century to Confederation in the nineteenth, had as its central idea the uniting of a French and an English community on a basis that guaranteed some cultural integrity for both.

Historically, the Tories stood for the supremacy of the crown and the established church, and for a society closely connected with the land. Conservatives in both Britain and Canada are called Tories, but the real Tories were pre-Conservative: they revolved around a domestic economy and a personal relationship to the working class that was destroyed by the Industrial Revolution. Expressions of Canadian opposition to American ideology, all through the nineteenth century, attack from the left quite as often as from the right. One writer, in 1841, spoke of "the United States, where from the great mixture of races, British feelings and British connexion have given way before a flood of undefinable notions about liberty and equality, mixed with aristocratic wealth, slavery, and bigotry in religion". I quote this not because it is profound but because it is commonplace; and we notice that what the writer dislikes is not only American democracy but American oligarchy, the inequalities of wealth and opportunity. It is not surprising, then, that so many of Canada's intellectuals, both English and French, should be one form or another of Tory radical. One of these, and also one of the ablest commentators on the Canadian scene, George Grant, writes near the end of his *Lament for a Nation*:

> The impossibility of conservatism in our era is the impossibility of Canada. As Canadians we attempted a ridiculous task in trying to build a conservative nation in the age of progress, on a continent we share with the most dynamic nation on earth. The current of modern history was against us.

Yet before we write off Canada as an abortive and quixotic culture that has failed to break through the heavy snow-crust of a technological world, it might be worth asking what there is, in this Tory devotion to crown and church and land, that can be translated into terms of the nineteen-seventies. Human ideas have an extraordinary power of metamorphosis, and many things that are outdated or absurd in their original context may reappear later in a very different aspect. For instance, no church has ever been established in Canada, but there has been a much closer connexion between church and state, especially in education, which has given Canadian culture a distinctive coloring. Again, there may be advantages in having the personal symbol of the Queen instead of the impersonal one of the flag, which Canada did not have until recently, and would hardly miss if it still did not. But I think something rather different is involved here, which I shall illustrate by an example. When I first came to Toronto, in 1929, it was a homogeneous Scotch-Irish town, dominated by the Orange Order, and greatly derided by the rest of Canada for its smugness, its snobbery, and its sterility. The public food in restaurants and hotels was of very indifferent quality, as it is in all right-thinking Anglo-Saxon communities. After the war, Toronto took in immigrants to the extent of nearly a quarter of its population, and large Greek, Italian, Portuguese, Central European, West Indian communities grew up within it. The public food improved dramatically. More important, these communities all seemed to find their own place in the larger community with a minimum of violence and tension, preserving much of their own cultures and yet taking part in the total one. It has always seemed to me that this very relaxed absorption of minorities, where there is no concerted effort at a "melting pot", has something to do with what the Queen symbolizes, the separation of the head of state from the head of government. Because Canada was founded by two peoples, nobody could ever know what a hundred per cent Canadian was, and hence the decentralizing rhythm that is so essential to culture had room to expand.

Still more important is the Canadian sense of the close relation of the people to the land. Everywhere we turn in Canadian literature and painting, we are haunted by the natural world, and even the most sophisticated Canadian artists can hardly keep something very primitive and archaic out of their imaginations. This sense is not that of the possession of the land, but precisely the absence of possession, a feeling that here is a nature that man has polluted and imprisoned and violated but has never really lived with.

Canada does not have quite so heavy a burden of guilt toward red and black peoples as the United States, and the French record with the Indians was rather better than the British or Spanish record. Even so there is little to be proud of: in Newfoundland, for instance, a gentle and inoffensive people, the Beothuks, were exterminated as casually as though they were mosquitoes. But still the main focus of guilt in Canada seems to fall on the rape of nature. The deaths of animals seems to have an extraordinary resonance in Canadian literature, as though the screams of all the trapped and tortured creatures who built up the Canadian fur trade were still echoing in our minds. One of the silliest of Tory fetishes, the preserving of game, seems to be taking a very different role in the Canadian imagination.

The seventeenth-century invaders of both countries brought with them the Cartesian ego, the sense of man as a perceiving subject, totally different from everything else in nature by virtue of his consciousness. It was a long time before the philosophers got around to realizing that egocentric consciousness is primarily a consciousness of death, but the poets had always known that: even the nineteenth-century rhetorical poets I spoke of wrote their best poetry in elegiac or nostalgic or other moods that were close to the sense of death. The narrative poets gave us stories of death in log jams, on glaciers, in hunting expeditions where the hunter seems to identify with his victim. This was not of course confined to Canada: one thinks of Whitman, who also wrote his best poetry about death and his worst rhetoric about democracy. But it was so strong in Canada as to give most of its serious literature, especially its poetry, a very sombre cast.

In 1948 a group of Quebec artists, headed by Paul-Emile Borduas, produced a surrealist manifesto called *Refus Global*, which seems to me a most important break-through in Canadian culture, not because of what it said, which was naive and confused enough, but because it was a sign that the old antithesis between a conscious mind and an unconscious nature was breaking down. For Borduas, the human mind contained an It as well as an I or ego, and this It was what he felt needed expression. In more recent painting, in the quasi-realism of Alex Colville and Christopher Pratt, in the ghostly figures of Jean-Paul Lemieux, there is often a feeling of loneliness and emptiness, as though the conscious mind were deliberately draining itself of its contents, and waiting for something else to move in. Meanwhile an interest in Indian and Eskimo art, with all their nature-spirits, has grown into a fascination, and many of our younger poets — Susan Musgrave, John Newlove, Gwendolyn MacEwen — write as though Indians and Eskimos were our direct cultural ancestors whose traditions continue in them and in us. In fiction, there are some curious stories, such as Margaret Atwood's *Surfacing* and Marian Engel's *Bear*, of heroines turning away from their civilized heritage toward an identity with nature. It seems clear that for Canadian culture the old imperialist phrase "going native" has come home to roost. We are no longer an army of occupation, and the natives are ourselves.

The first half of the twentieth century saw a bitter dispute between democratic and Marxist conceptions of the best way to minimize the exploitation of man by man. Nobody seemed to notice that both sides were exploiting nature with equal recklessness. It seems to me that the capitalist-socialist controversy is out of date, and that a détente with an outraged nature is what is important now. Canada is still a place of considerable natural resources, but it is no longer simply a place to be looted, either by Canadians or by non-Canadians. It is of immense importance to the United States itself that there should be other views of the human occupation of this continent, rooted in different ideologies and different historical traditions. And it is of immense importance to the world that a country which used to be at the edge of the earth and is now a kind of global Switzerland, surrounded by all the world's great powers, should have achieved the repatriating of its culture. For this is essentially what has happened in the last twenty years, in all parts of Canada; and what was an inarticulate space on a map is now responding to the world with the tongues and eyes of a matured and disciplined imagination.

"Conclusion" to
Literary History of Canada

Second Edition

It is difficult to know what to say, as a general conclusion, to this part of the *Literary History* that is not already said or implied in my previous conclusion. Ten or twelve years is not a generation, much less, even in these future-shock days, a historical period. The logical starting point, I think, has to be the reason for producing a volume of this size so few years after the original one, and the reason is not difficult to grasp. Mr Cross, writing on history, says that five hundred books in that field were produced during five of the years he covers; Mr Woodcock counts over a thousand volumes of verse, excluding anthologies; nearly every contributor says or implies something about the colossal verbal explosion that has taken place in Canada since 1960. Such a quantitative increase eventually makes for a qualitative change: this change cannot, in so short a time, reveal much essentially new to the critical observer, but it does mean that the trends I studied in the previous conclusion have reached something of a crisis since then. All I can do here is to try to characterize that crisis: there can be no question of attempting any rounded general survey of the period.

Our reviewers are comprehensive to the verge of omni-science, and with all their selectivity they have little space to do more than mention a great number of books which are not simply entertaining, interesting, or instructive, but are richly rewarding to read. Such critical comments as they are able to make are often tantalizingly brief, like Mr New's remark about the influence of structuralism and linguistics on the prose style of Canadian fiction. The fact that the book is something of a catalogue is nothing against it, but is on the contrary essential to its usefulness. Part of the total verbal explosion is the information explosion, and one of the more efficient ways of trying to cope with that is the 'review of recent scholarship' article, a genre which this book closely approximates.

Critical methods, confronting such an avalanche of material, have to become rather more subtle than they were in the old days of collecting Canadians, putting the authentic specimens of Loyalist descent (or 'stock,' in the E.K. Broadus anthology) in the centre of a penumbra of immigrant, expatriate, transient, and tourist writers, some of whom, like Grove and Grey Owl, turned out to be masks of quite different people. The mask in Canadian literature would make a good thesis for somebody, and doubtless has done. Twenty years ago, the Canadian critical scene was full of schools and orthodoxies and heresies and divergences and conflicting theories, the prevalence of which, in literary criticism no less than in religion or psychology, indicates a general failure to understand what is being talked about. It would be an affectation for me to pretend not to notice that I am extensively featured in this book myself, and among the many things I am grateful for and deeply appreciate, one is the fact that the phrase 'the Frye school of mythopoeic poetry' is so briefly dismissed by Mr Woodcock. There is no Frye school of mythopoeic poetry; criticism and poetry cannot possibly be related in that way; the myth of a poem is the structural principle of that poem, and consequently all poems that make any sense at all are equally mythopoeic, and so on and so on: the phrase, as Borges remarks about something in Fichte, is almost inexhaustibly fallacious. The concreteness of this book, the absence of anxiety and special pleading, the constant awareness of the genuine authority of the literature the reviewer is dealing with, is reflected in the literature itself. Mr Bissell notes that a good deal of recent political writing, even when strongly partisan, shows a real concern for objectivity and respect for facts; and similarly, the thesis novel, the assertive poem, the rib-nudging allegory, the assumption that literature can be 'effective' only when it turns into sub-literary rhetoric, seem to be receding from the literary scene.

For well over a century, and years before the satire in *Grip* that Mr Pacey quotes, discussions about Canadian literature usually took the form of the shopper's dialogue: 'Have you any Canadian literature today?' 'Well, we're expecting something in very shortly.' But that age is over, and writing this conclusion gives me rather the feeling of driving a last spike, of waking up from the National Neurosis. There is much more to come, just as there were all those CPR trains still to come, but Canadian literature is here, perhaps still a minor but certainly no longer a gleam in a paternal critic's eye. It is a typically Canadian irony that such a cataract started pouring out of the presses just before Marshall McLuhan became the most famous of Canadian critics for saying that the book was finished. I doubt if one can find this in McLuhan, except by quoting him irresponsibly out of context, but it is what he was widely believed to have said, and the assertion became very popular, as anything that sounds anti-intellectual always does. Abandoning irony, one may say that a population the size of English-writing Canada, subject to all the handicaps which have been chronicled so often in Canadian criticism, does not produce such a bulk of good writing without an extraordinary vitality and morale behind it. At the same time, to achieve, to bring a future into the present, is also to become finite, and the sense of that is always a little disconcerting, even though becoming finite means becoming genuinely human.

Canadians, as I have implied, have a highly developed sense of irony, but even so, De Gaulle's monumental gaffe of 1967, 'vive le Québec libre,' is one of the great ironic remarks in Canadian history, because it was hailing the emergence of precisely the force that Quebec had really got free from. For the Quiet Revolution was as impressive an achievement of imaginative freedom as the contemporary world can show: freedom not so much from clerical domination or corrupt politics as from the burden of tradition. The whole *je me souviens* complex in French Canada, the anxiety of resisting change, the strong emotionalism which was, as emotion by itself always is, geared to the past: this was what Quebec had shaken off to such an astonishing degree. It was accompanied, naturally enough, by intense anti-English and separatist feelings, which among the more confused took the form that De Gaulle was interested in, a French neo-colonialism. This last is dead already; separatism is still a strong force, and will doubtless remain one for some time, but one gets the feeling that it is being inexorably bypassed by history, and that even if it achieves its aims it will do so in a historical vacuum. I begin with French Canada because it seems to me that the decisive cultural event in English Canada during the past fifteen years has been the impact of French Canada and its new sense of identity. After so long and so obsessive a preoccupation with the same subject, it took the Quiet Revolution to create a real feeling of identity in English Canada, and to make cultural nationalism, if that is the best phrase, a genuine force in the country, even a bigger and more significant one than economic nationalism, which is, as Mr Mayo notes, mainly a Central Canada movement.

The immense power of American penetration into Canada is traditionally thought of as either economic or sub-cultural: Canadians buy American cars and watch American situation comedies on television. Without denying the importance of these phenomena, in the last decade there has been a considerable growth of emphasis on more genuinely cultural aspects. This emphasis has affected Canadian attitudes to the publishing business, to the Canadian editions of *Time* and the *Reader's Digest*, to American television programs brought in, with their advertising, by cable, and to many other things: but perhaps the most widely publicized issue has been that of American appointments to Canadian universities. The reactions to these, proposals for quota systems and the like, may be theoretically untenable and practically impotent, but the kind of problem they try to meet is not an unreal one. Academics of course are a conservative breed, and they still try to keep explaining to one another that scholarship knows no boundaries. Scholarship may not, but culture does: and the only reason for having scholarship is that it is necessary to culture.

I am not a continentalist myself, although I have been called one, and I can see that in the later work of Underhill, for instance, a writer whom of course I deeply respect and have learned much from, a naïve admiration for things American amounts almost to a betrayal of his own liberalism. An independent Canada would be much more useful to the United States itself than a dependent or annexed one would be, and it is of great importance to the United States to have a critical view of it centred in Canada, a view which is not hostile but is simply another view. The United States has its share of fools like other countries, and just as fifty years ago senators would propose that Britain hand over Canada in payment of her war debt, so there are senators and others now (see Mr Chapman's article) who tell us how lovely it would be if we placed all our resources unquestioningly in American hands. Resistance to such things is in the United States' own best interests. The nationalism that has evolved in Canada is on the whole a positive development, in which self-awareness has been far more important than aggressiveness. Perhaps identity only is identity when it becomes, not militant, but a way of defining oneself against something else. In any case problems of culture and of verbal articulation are the primary concern of this book. I see the kind of creative vitality which this book records as an emerging form of Canadian self-definition, and that involves looking at the difference from the American parallel development. The word 'parallel' is important: Canada may be an American colony, as is often said, by me among others, but Canadians have never thought of the United States as a parental figure, like Britain, and analogies of youthful revolt and the like would be absurd.

To begin with a different kind of analogy: in countries where Marxism has not come to power, but where there is a strong Marxist minority, we see what an advantage it is to have a unified conceptual structure that can be applied to practically anything. It may often distort what it is applied to, but that matters less than the tactical advantage of having it. Defenders of more empirical points of view find their battlefronts disintegrating into separate and isolated outposts. They may demonstrate that this or that point is wrong, but such rearguard actions lack glamour. The same principle can be applied to the pragmatic, compromising, ad hoc, ramshackle Canadian tradition vis-à-vis the far more integrated and revolutionary American one. The coherence of the 'American way of life' is often underestimated by Americans themselves, because the more thoughtful citizens of any country are likely to be more preoccupied with its anomalies. Hence outsiders, including Canadians, may find the consistency easier to see. De Tocqueville, who didn't like much of what he saw in the United

States, wrote his book very largely about that consistency, almost in spite of himself.

As Canada and the United States went their separate ways on the same continent, eventually coming to speak for the most part the same language, their histories took on a strong pattern of contrast. The United States found its identity in the eighteenth century, the age of rationalism and enlightenment. It retains a strong intellectual fascination with the eighteenth century: its founding fathers are still its primary cultural heroes, and the bicentenary celebrations of 1976, from all accounts, will be mainly celebrations of the eighteenth century rather than of the present day. The eighteenth-century cultural pattern took on a revolutionary, and therefore a deductive, shape, provided with a manifesto of independence and a written constitution. This in turn developed a rational attitude to the continuity of life in time, and this attitude seems to me the central principle of the American way of life. The best image for it is perhaps that of the express train. It is a conception of progress, but of progress defined by mechanical rather than organic metaphors, and hence the affinity with the eighteenth century is not really historical: it tends in fact to be anti-historical. Washington, Franklin, Jefferson, with their imperturbable common sense, are thought of, in the popular consciousness, more as deceased contemporaries than as ancestors living among different cultural referents. The past is thus assimilated to the present, a series of stations that our express train has stopped at and gone beyond.

In law and politics, new situations are met by reinterpreting, or in the last resort amending, an eighteenth-century document: proceeding, in other words, in a deductive direction, giving priority to the kind of logic which most clearly represents the mechanics of thought. In economics, there has been, and with qualifications there still is, a strong belief in laissez-faire, as a continuous and semi-autonomous process that will work by itself if left alone. The most characteristic American philosophical attitude is the pragmatism, so different from Canadian pragmatism, which sees truth as emerging from a course of consistent action. Its most characteristic attitude to education is the anti-contemplative Dewey conception of learning through doing, or, again, through continuous activity. In religion, the real established church in the United States is that of eighteenth-century deism, where God is the umpire behind the competing churches, leaving man to justify himself by the continuity of his good works, which include the separating of church from state and the secularizing of education.

In attempting to characterize such a central driving force, one is bound to oversimplify and ignore powerful counter-forces. The United States is full of people deeply opposed to the attitudes I call characteristic. I see these attitudes, however, as symbols of something which has so far proved flexible enough to contain and absorb those counter-forces, greatly modifying itself as it has done so, but becoming stronger in consequence, and hence still in the driver's seat. What I am trying to describe cannot be reduced to a cliché, like the 'Consciousness One' of *The Greening of America*, or the naïve optimism that perished with the 1929 crash, or a simple-minded trust in technology, much less 'materialism,' or a 'worship of the almighty dollar.' The traumas of Vietnam and Watergate have another side. The original impulse to go into Vietnam was part of a quite genuine political belief which, as a belief, is still there; and what carried public morale through the sickening revelations of Watergate was a loyalty to the constitutional tradition, which still functions much as the Torah does for Judaism. In the beginning the Americans created America, and America is the beginning of the world. That is, it is the oldest country in the world: no other nation's history goes back so far with less social metamorphosis. Through all the anxieties and doubts of recent years one can still hear the confident tones of its Book of Genesis: 'We hold these truths to be self-evident.' At least a Canadian can hear them, because nothing has ever been self-evident in Canada.

Canada had no enlightenment, and very little eighteenth century. The British and French spent the eighteenth century in Canada battering down each other's forts, and Canada went directly from the Baroque expansion of the seventeenth century to the Romantic expansion of the nineteenth. The result was the cultural situation that I tried to characterize in my earlier conclusion. Identity in Canada has always had something about it of a centrifugal movement into far distance, of clothes on a growing giant coming apart at the seams, of an elastic about to snap. Stephen Leacock's famous hero who rode off rapidly in all directions was unmistakably a Canadian. This expanding

movement has to be counterbalanced by a sense of having constantly to stay together by making tremendous voluntary efforts at
intercommunication, whether of building the CPR or of holding
federal-provincial conferences.

There is a novel called *Canadian Born*, by Mrs Humphry
Ward, written about 1908. In the opening pages we meet the
heroine, Lady Merton, an Englishwoman whose father is
important enough for her to be travelling across Canada in a
private railway car. They are held up by a 'sink-hole,' described as
'a place where you can't find no bottom,' and which ten train-
loads of dumping has failed to fill. Still, Lady Merton is deeply
impressed with what she sees of 'the march of a new people to its
home,' especially after she meets an attractive Canadian male, and
says to a less enthusiastic Britisher, 'Don't you feel that we must get
the natives to guide us — to put us in the way? It is only they who
can really feel the poetry of it all.' She later says: '*We* see the drama
— we feel it — much more than they can who are in it,' and quotes
Matthew Arnold: 'On to the bound of the waste — on to the City of
God!'

The author is a keen and intelligent observer, and her view of
Canada in 1908 is consistent with many other contemporary views
of it. She is also trying hard not to be patronizing. Nevertheless the
great march of a new people can be seen better by visitors from
higher civilizations, and the natives, poor sods, can only feel (not
write) the poetry of it all. They may be headed for the City of God,
but it is a very long way to the bound of the waste, and in the
meantime there is that sink-hole. She has caught one of the essential Canadian moods, the feeling of apology for being so huge and
tedious an obstacle on the way to somewhere more interesting,
whether the City of God, the glittering treasures of the Orient, or
the opulent United States. It seems to me very characteristic of
Canada that its highest Order should have for its motto: 'looking
for a better country.' The quotation is from the New Testament,
where the better country really is the City of God, but the feeling it
expresses has more mundane contexts.

Such feelings of insecurity and inferiority are still with us:
the brain drain has eased considerably, but there is the more
serious issue raised in J.J. Brown's *Ideas in Exile*, referred to by Mr
Chapman; and we still force pastoral myths on our children
designed to reassure their elders, according to Miss Egoff. But

transitions to something different are marked in this book. Some of the articles deal with non-literary subjects, and there, what is important, for the present context, is not that many Canadians are distinguished chemists or engineers or whatever, but that all the non-literary subjects have their role to play in creating the imaginative climate that this book is trying to put into isobars. If we look at Mr Swinton's chapter, for instance, we see that there is no such thing as 'Canadian biology': the phrase makes no sense. But the fact that Canada was, a couple of generations ago, regarded as possessed of 'unlimited natural resources,' and the later pricking of that gaseous balloon, gives biology a distinctive resonance in Canadian cultural life, and helps, for instance, to make Farley Mowat one of our best-known and best-selling authors. Much the same is true of the intense Canadian interest in geology and geophysics, reflected in Mr Chapman's account of Tuzo Wilson. I have often thought that Robert Frost's line, 'The land was ours before we were the land's,' however appropriate to the United States, does not apply to Canada, where the opposite seems to me to have been true, even in the free land grant days. Canadians were held by the land before they emerged as a people on it, a land with its sinister aspects, or what Warren Tallman, referred to by Mr Ross, calls the 'gray wolf,' but with its fostering aspects too, of the kind that come into the phrase of Alice Wilson which one is grateful to Mr Swinton for quoting: 'the earth touches every life.'

Many of these themes illustrate the importance in Canada of the theme of survival, the title of Margaret Atwood's very influential book which is, as Mr Pacey says, a most perceptive essay on an aspect of the Canadian sensibility. Mr Ross points out some of its limitations: it does not have, and was clearly not intended to have, the kind of comprehensiveness that a conceptual thesis, like the frontier theory in American history, would need. But it is not simply saying that Canadians are a nation of losers. What the author means by survival comes out more clearly, I think, in her extraordinary novel *Surfacing*, where the heroine is isolated from her small group and finds something very archaic, both inside and outside her, taking over her identity. The word survival implies living through a series of crises, each one unexpected and different from the others, each one to be met on its own terms. Failure to meet the crisis means that some death principle moves in. From Mr Goudge we learn that the theme of survival has had some odd extensions in Canadian philosophy: death itself may be simply one more discontinuity in existence.

This discontinuous sense of life is obviously a contrast to the American sense of continuity, and it affords more scope for the tragic, as distinct from the ironic, mood in Canadian literature. American fiction is prevailingly ironic for many reasons, but one reason is that irony (as a mode of fiction, not as an attitude) fits the American continuous perspective: it presents life as a horizontal continuum which stops rather than ends, like a car which may or may not go into the ditch but has run out of gas anyway. In tragedy, however dingy the hero may be, there is a fall through time, a polarizing of two levels of existence. They are equally valid forms, but there is a great deal more facile irony than facile tragedy, and the standard ironic formulas, the Slow Strangle, the Ouroboros, or Biting Oneself in the Tail, the Hateful Self-Discovery, are often used rather perfunctorily, as symbols of a serious literary intention. Tragic narratives are more structured, formalized, even contrived, reflecting as they so often do the sense of contrivance in outward circumstances. The affinity with the tragic is part of the affinity with formalism in Canadian writing, and both may be connected with the sense of discontinuity, the feeling for sudden descent or catastrophe, that seems to me to have an unusual emphasis in Canada.

The theme of descent may be as astringent as it is in *Surfacing* or as genial as in Robertson Davies' *Manticore*, where it takes the form of a Jungian analysis followed by images of caves and bears. But in the Zurich clinic, no less than in the Quebec forest, there is still something of the 'gray wolf,' even of the sink-hole. In the fall of the hero of David Knight's tightly constructed Nigerian story, *Farquharson's Physique*, in the Donnelly massacre at the end of Reaney's trilogy, in the writhings of Margaret Laurence's Hagar and Rachel (Mr New points out the importance of the perspective on time in *The Stone Angel*), we realize that we are still in the country of Grove and Pratt. Some contributors have commented on the tragic tone of George Grant's *Lament for a Nation* and Creighton's *Canada's First Century*: the interest of such books does not end with the issues they deal with, because the tragic is always a major aspect of the human situation. Still, one may hope for a writer of equal power who will see a structure of comedy also in the Canadian story.

If we look at the three eighteenth-century events that defined the future of Canada (as of so much else in the modern world), the Quebec Act, the American Revolution, and the French Revolution, we see the whole range of a political spectrum that still confronts us. The Quebec Act came close to an Edmund Burke model: it was an inductive, pragmatic recognition of a de facto situation, and the situation was one of those profoundly illogical ones that Burke considered typical of human life generally. The two factors to be taken into account were: (a) the British have conquered the French (b) the British have done nothing of the kind. The only way out of this was a settlement that guaranteed some rights to both parties. The French Revolution, proceeding deductively from general principles, was what Burke condemned so bitterly as 'metaphysical,' and was also the forerunner of the dialectical Marxist revolutions. The American Revolution came in the middle, a strong contrast to the Canadian settlement, as we have seen, but keeping far more of the broadening-through-precedent British tradition than the French one did.

Hence although the United States itself got started on a revolutionary basis, it was a basis of a kind that made it difficult for that country to come to terms with the later Marxist revolutions. This produced a growing isolation from other revolutionary ideologies and societies, the climax of which was the maintaining, for so many years, of the grotesque fantasy that the refugee army in Formosa was the government of China. At the same time, the 'melting pot' assumptions of the nineteenth-century United States, the ambition described in the inscription on the Statue of Liberty of making a united democracy out of the most varied social and racial elements, became profoundly modified. The conception of the 'hundred per cent American' has been succeeded by a growing feeling that the various elements in American society can perhaps contribute more to it by retaining something of their original cultural characteristics. Here there is a growing similarity to the Canadian pattern, where the necessity of recognizing two major social elements at the beginning meant that nobody could ever possibly know what a 'hundred per cent Canadian' was, and hence led to a much more relaxed ideal of a national 'melting pot.'

When the last edition of this book was published, the centenary of Canadian Confederation was coming up: the bicentenary of the

American Revolution is the corresponding event on this horizon, if an anniversary is an event. It seems to me that a very curious and significant exchange of identities between Canada and the United States has taken place since then. The latter, traditionally so buoyant, extroverted, and forward-looking, appears to be entering a prolonged period of self-examination. I am setting down very subjective impressions here, derived mainly from what little I know of American literature and literary criticism, but I feel that a search for a more genuinely historical dimension of consciousness has been emerging at least since Vietnam turned into a nightmare, and is still continuing. Part of it is a different attitude to the past, a re-examining of it to see what things went wrong when. This is not simply a reversing of the current of continuity, like a psychiatric patient exploring his childhood: there seems to be a growing tendency to think more in terms of inevitable discontinuities. Erik Erikson's book on identity, an attempt to clarify the psychology of the disturbances of a few years ago, is an example.

Another part of the re-examination, and imaginatively perhaps the more significant part, revolves around the question: has the American empire, like the British empire before it, simply passed its climacteric and is it now declining, or at least becoming aware of limits? If so, the past takes on a rise-and-fall parabola shape, not a horizontal line in which the past is on the same plane as the present. This may not sound like much on paper, but changes in central metaphors and conceptual diagrams are symbolic of the most profound disturbances that the human consciousness has to face. After the strident noise and confusion of the later sixties, there was, for all the discussion, an eerie quietness about the response to Watergate, and to the irony of a President's turning into a cleaned-out gambler a few months after getting an overwhelming mandate. Even the violence of the now almost unmanageable cities seems to have caused less panic than one might reasonably have expected. Perhaps it is not too presumptuous to say, although few non-Canadian readers would understand what was meant, that the American way of life is slowly becoming Canadianized.

Meanwhile, Canada, traditionally so diffident, introverted, past-and-future fixated, incoherent, inarticulate, proceeding by hunch and feeling, seems to be taking on, at least culturally, an inner composure and integration of outlook, even some buoyancy

and confidence. The most obvious reasons for this are technological. The airplane and the television set, in particular, have
brought a physical simultaneity into the country that has greatly
modified the older, and perhaps still underlying, blazed-trail and
canoe mentality. As Mr Cross says, we are now in a post-
Laurentian phase of development. In the railway days, being a
federal MP from British Columbia or a literary scholar in Alberta
required an intense, almost romantic, commitment, because of the
investment of time and energy involved in getting from such
places to the distant centres that complemented them. Today such
things are jobs like other jobs, and the relation to the primary
community has assumed a correspondingly greater importance.
This is the positive and creative side of the relaxing of centralizing
tensions in modern society, of which separatism represents a less
creative one.

The influence of television is often blamed for violence, and
certainly there are television programs that are profoundly dis-
tasteful from this point of view. But there is another side to television: bringing the remote into our living room can be a very
sobering form of communication, and a genuinely humanizing
one. I remember the thirties, when so many 'intellectuals' were
trying to rationalize or ignore the Stalin massacres or whatever
such horrors did not fit their categories, and thinking even then
that part of their infantilism was in being men of print: they saw
only lines of type on a page, not lines of prisoners shuffling off to
death camps. But something of the real evil of the Vietnam war did
get on television, and the effect seems to have been on the whole a
healthy one. At least the American public came to hate the war,
instead of becoming complacent or inured to its atrocities.

Similarly in Canada: Eskimos, blacks, Indians, perhaps even
Wasps, cannot go on being comic-strip stereotypes after they have
been fully exposed on television. Of course better knowledge can
also create dislike and more tension; and when I speak of an
exchange of identities I certainly do not mean that Canada will
acquire anything of the simplistic optimism of an earlier age in
the United States. Television is one of many factors which will
make that impossible. Another is the curtailing of resources,
already mentioned. Still another is the emergence of chilling technical possibilities in genetics, which raise questions about identity
that make our traditional ones look like learning to spell cat.

Another is the geography of the global village. In the nineteenth century the Canadian imagination responded to the Biblical phrase 'from the river unto the ends of the earth,' and one of the historians referred to by Mr Cross, W.L. Morton, has written with great sensitivity about the impact, psychological and otherwise, of the northern frontier on the Canadian consciousness. But now Canada has become a kind of global Switzerland, surrounded by the United States on the south, the European common market on the east, the Soviet Union on the north, China and Japan on the west.

In some essays in this book a distinctive Canadian bias shows through that may be culturally significant. The fact that Descartes is a French philosopher is not simply a biographical fact: Descartes is French in the sense that he is a permanent and central part of a tradition that makes France different in its cultural pattern from other countries. Similarly with Locke as a British philosopher, or Kant as a German one, or William James as an American one. Canada seems to have no philosopher of this defining kind: what Canadian philosophy does have is a strong emphasis on religion, so remarkable as to be worth pausing on for a moment.

Mr Goudge, writing of philosophy, is compelled to deal with religion even though there is a separate chapter on religion; the only cult-philosopher in the country, Bernard Lonergan, referred to by Mr Grant, is a religious philosopher; much is said in this book and elsewhere about the religious drive in George Grant, in McLuhan, in myself. In Creighton the drive may not be technically religious, but it is certainly prophetic. Here again French Canada established a pattern which English Canada to some degree imitated, of keeping church and state closer together, particularly in education, than was done in the United States. Mr Grant's urbane treatment of ecumenical movements in Canada makes it clear that while religion is ideally a uniting force in society, it is more likely in practice to be a divisive one. Religion in Canada has closely followed the centrifugal and expanding rhythm of Canadian life, spearheaded by missionaries, from the seventeenth-century Jesuits to our own time — even Norman Bethune was a missionary in a sense. As it did so an intensely competitive spirit developed, as we can see if we walk through any Canadian town. The centrifugal movement came to a halt when the population started rolling back into the growing cities, and the urbanizing of Canadian mores greatly weakened the social influence of the churches, which long remained fixated on the earlier social values. The temperance movement, for example, as we find it in, say, Nellie McClung, was often associated with a very genuine political liberalism, even radicalism, in nineteenth-century Canada, but the growth of cities turned it into a horse-and-buggy phenomenon that could rouse no response except ridicule.

There is nothing here sociologically different from what happened in the United States, but the comparative absence of what I have called American deism may have made the impact of religion on the Canadian consciousness more direct. I remember a Spring Thaw skit of some years ago, where a Roman Catholic, an Anglican, and a United Church leader sang a song about charity and brotherly love, then each in turn, after glancing darkly at his confrères, stepped forward and informed the audience that of course *he* was God's accredited spokesman. The audience found the skit very funny, but I recall someone remarking that possibly only a Canadian audience would have done so.

I had long realized that the religious context of so many Canadian intellectuals had something to do with the peripheral situation of Canada, in the way that, for instance, Denmark was an appropriate place for a Kierkegaard in nineteenth-century Europe. Kierkegaard's hostility to what he called 'Christendom' had a lot to do with the impact of the mores of bigger countries on his own. When I read Mr Woodcock on the role of the Canadian poet as a counter-culture hero, something else rang a bell, and enabled me to make a connection with literature.

Canada has always been a cool climate for heroes: Mr Bissell speaks of the grudging support given to our last three prime ministers, all of whom, whatever one thinks of their policies, have compared very favourably, in intelligence and personal integrity, with some of those who adorned the White House in the same period; and Mrs Thomas's survey of Canadian biography reveals very little response in Canada to any Carlylean great-man conception of history. It would be interesting, and very typical of Canada, if Canadian literature had found its soul, so to speak, by defining the poet as a counter-hero or anti-hero. Of course this counter-cultural aspect of poetry is true of the United States also; but it seems to me that Canada has been steadily building up something like a North American counter-culture against the United States which is now big and complex enough to be examined on its own terms. Once more, 'against' simply means differentiation.

It may be the end of the century before any real coherence will emerge from our cultural pattern: so far we are confined to what Eliot would call hints followed by guesses. But some things in the Canadian tradition are beginning to look very international. It seems to me that in the democracies generally today, the dialectical habit of mind is giving way to a tendency to think in containing terms, where the antithesis is included and absorbed instead of being defined by exclusion. This is really a conservative tendency in thought, although not directly connected with political conservatism: Mr Bissell quotes an example of it from Abraham Rotstein, who is very far from being a right-winger. At the same time, as we can see if we look carefully at what Mr Cross has to say about W.L. Morton, W.J. Eccles, and Carl Berger in particular, the tendency is conservative, in the sense of revolving around the question of what it is necessary or important to conserve. As such, it is a tendency that fulfils the tradition of Burke in Canada, in which opposition forms a larger synthesis instead of an apocalyptic separation of sheep and goats. The anti-Marxist attitude of mind suggested here, if I am right about it, is one of crucial importance for literature, in Canada and elsewhere. Marxism is a very remarkable intellectual achievement as well as the dominant moral force in the contemporary world, but, at least wherever it has come to power, it cannot really cope with the humanities or with the place of the arts in modern society.

When I read through the more purely literary chapters of this book, and check them against my own meagre first-hand knowledge, I am struck by a feature of Canadian writing that seems to me a literary parallel to the conservative tendency just spoken of. It might be called formalism or even classicism: I should prefer, however, to call it simply professionalism. Modern society has decreed that very few writers shall live by paper alone, and the great majority of our writers are part-time writers, but that is not what I mean. I mean writing from within literature and within its genres, as opposed to the 'I've got something important to say' approach of the amateur, who then looks around for a fictional or poetic vehicle to put his important say into. The professional attitude has affinities, if we like, with the principle that the medium is the message. I should say rather that in fully realized writing there is no difference between structure and content, what is called content being the structure of the individual work, as distinct from the structure of the convention or genre to which it belongs.

Professionalism means technique and craftsmanship, which amateur writers often think of as a weakening of the moral fibre. Canadian criticism has been plagued a good deal by the foolish notion that imagination is a by-product of extremes, specifically emotional extremes. We can't have a great literature in Canada because we're too safe, sane, dull, humdrum — not enough lynchings, one critic suggested. The professional writer discovers from his experience that the imagination is the constructive element in the mind, and that intensity cannot be conveyed except through structure, which includes design, balance, and proportion. Of all genres, this is perhaps most obvious in the drama, where the show has to go over or else, and Mr Ripley has some trenchant observations about the importance of a professional attitude in the theatre.

Once technique reaches a certain degree of skill, it turns into something that we may darkly suspect to be fun: fun for the writer to display it, fun for the reader to watch it. In the old days we were conditioned to believe that only lowbrows read for fun, and that highbrows read serious literature to improve their minds. The coming of radio did a good deal to help this morbid situation, and television has done something (not enough) more. We now live in a time when Leonard Cohen can start out with an erudite book of poems called *Let Us Compare Mythologies*, the chief mythologies being the Biblical and the Classical, and evolve from there, quite naturally, into a well-known folk singer. Mr Woodcock points out the immense importance of the revival of the oral tradition, the public speaking of poetry to audiences, often with a background of music, in making the serious poet a genuinely popular figure.

To be popular means having the power to amuse, in a genuine sense, and the power to amuse is, again, dependent on skill and craftsmanship. Mr Woodcock speaks of an element in Earle Birney's poetry that might almost be called stunting, an interest in every variety of technical experiment, as though experiment were an end in itself. This is not a matter of panting to keep up with all the avant-garde movements: Birney is a genuinely contemporary poet, and his versatility expresses a central contemporary interest. Mr Lane refers to the zany quality in Marshall McLuhan's style that has infuriated some people into calling him a humbug and a charlatan. James Reaney writes plays, sometimes tragic ones, full of the let's-pretend devices of children's games, devices which, if they were described out of their context, might sound like Peter Quince and his wall in *A Midsummer Night's Dream*. The verbal wit that comes through in, say, Leonard Cohen's *Beautiful Losers*, in some of Needham's essays (see Mr Conron's article), in the concrete poets, is a sign of the presence of seriousness and not the absence of it, the serious being the opposite of the solemn. We are a long way from the days when a bewildered Joyce, confronted with responses to *Finnegans Wake* which invariably treated it with either awe or ridicule, said: 'But why couldn't they see that the book was funny?'

About twenty years ago I started trying to explain that the poet *qua* poet had no notion of life or reality or experience until he had read enough poetry to understand from it how poetry dealt with such things. I was told, in all quarters from Canadian journals (see Mr Ross's article) to university classrooms, that I was reducing literature to a verbal game. I would not accept the word 'reducing,' but otherwise the statement was correct enough. Now that the work ethic has settled into a better perspective, the play ethic is also coming into focus, and we can perhaps understand a bit more clearly than we could a century ago why *Othello* and *Macbeth* are called plays. Play is that for the sake of which work is done, the climactic Sabbath vision of mankind.

A book concerned entirely with play in this sense passes over most of what occupies the emotional foreground of our lives at present: inflation, unemployment, violence and crime, and much else. The historian of Elizabethan literature, praising the exuberance and power of that literature, would not necessarily be unaware of the misery, injustice, and savagery that pervaded English life at the same time. What seems to come to matter more, eventually, is what man can create in the face of the chaos he also creates. This book is about what has been created, in words and in Canada, during the present age, and the whole body of that creation will be the main reason for whatever interest posterity may take in us.

II

Teaching

Teaching the Humanities Today

My first Modern Languages Association meeting was in 1947, in Detroit, and my experiences of it are still vivid in memory. I am at a group in Elizabethan literature where a young man reads a paper on the influence of Plato on Sidney's *Defence of Poesy*. At the end a senior scholar remarks that the parallels cited all come from the first book of Cicero's *De Oratore*. Then I am at a publisher's party with someone singing ballads to a guitar, my other ear exposed to the offer of a job with a department that appeared to spend most of its time hunting raccoons. The scene dissolves to a murky bar — in those days bars were as dark as the shade of Tiresias, doubtless to symbolize the more interesting aspects of sin. Various shapes looming out of the gloom prove to be editors of a journal of Catholic leanings, which in that generation meant that the name of St. Thomas Aquinas kept echoing like the chimes of Big Ben. Then I am passing through the hallways, and meet a glowering friend who says: "I haven't yet seen a single person here that I wanted to see". I overhear a remark: "Well, the trouble is that our board doesn't much like divorced people". I also overhear someone bursting with pride because a student of his had read a paper on a difficult word in *Beowulf* that had impressed the great Klaeber. One of the acts of the Executive Council in that year was to send an inscribed drinking mug to a baby who had been named Pamela after PMLA. In short, it was the same wonderful, ridiculous, exhilarating, crazy, endearing, exasperating experience that every MLA has been. Surely nothing else in modern civilization can be quite like it.

Still, it is becoming more of what it always was: I get letters expressing concern about the variety of offerings, and certainly a study of the programme does suggest an attempt to be all things to all men, even very nearly to all women. I think however that what is going on is not a circus midway but a genuine historical process. I have other memories of the Detroit meeting, of a different kind. I had come down from Toronto, and shared my hotel room, with Professor Barker Fairley, one of the finest Germanists of our time, who was reading a paper on Goethe. It was, I think, his last visit to the United States, as the cold-war hysteria set in shortly after, and, his wife being a left-winger, he was excluded from the country. He is ninety years old now, and is still excluded. And I remember how startled I was, as a Canadian unused to the ways of the United States thirty-odd years ago, to find in the hotel restaurant white waitresses in white uniforms and black bus-girls in yellow uniforms: a social distinction based on color which apparently no one objected to or even noticed. In 1977 the future is uncertain enough, but if there had been no sharpening of social awareness in the last thirty years it would be unimaginably worse.

The point of all this anecdotage is that the past is functional in our lives only when we neither forget it nor try to return to it. This is, of course, the principle on which the study of the humanities is also founded. Every work of literature meant something in its own day and now means something rather different to us. There is a constant illogical tension in criticism: we keep shuttling back and forth between historicity and relevance, the Elizabethan world-picture and Shakespeare our contemporary. But these two aspects of our work are not simply scholarly aspects: they involve two different, if complementary, conceptions of the university, of the society the university is in, and of our own relation to both.

When the MLA was founded, it took as its model the Classical-based humanism it was unconsciously displacing. Its creed, summarized in Arnold's *Culture and Anarchy*, ran something like this. Human experience is set in the frame of memory, and man's present life is fulfilled and completed by his past. The continuity of our cultural traditions gives dignity to our brief and muddled lives, and these traditions include the best that has been thought and said: that is, they include the vision of the greatest that man is capable of. In practice, the best is in the past, partly because it takes time before we can distinguish the best, and when we do distinguish it, we find that it often grows out of historical contexts very remote from us in their assumptions. Their remoteness helps to make them elements of a liberal, which means a liberating, education. The present cannot be an ideal object of knowledge like the past: as Ophelia says, we know what we are, but we know not what we may be. There is nothing liberating in merely seeing our own prejudices and stereotypes in a mirror, or in kidnapping the culture of the past to make it conform to them.

The legacy of the past is not, however, merely a tax-free inheritance added to our ordinary income. The best in the past, when liberated by the present, throws its shadow into the future, for whatever man has been capable of in imagination he can realize in life. In the future there is the possibility of an ideal society in which man's vision of his culture has liberated and equalized his social existence. The university which makes this vision possible forms a social counter-environment. We teach to give students an awareness of a greater freedom than society can give (the earliest MLAs showed a very genuine concern for teaching). We hold up to all students, whether casual or committed, the ideal of the scholarly life, a life detached yet not withdrawn from the social environment, working constantly, not to create an élite, but to dissolve all élites into the classless society which is the final embodiment of culture.

As our elders pursued this conception of scholarship, two things became obvious, and are very obviously reflected in this year's programme. One is that scholarship depends on knowledge, and the advance of knowledge is an advance in becoming unintelligible to more and more people. If I spend my life in an area of scholarship, I come to know something you don't know; or, if you do know it, you're in my in-group and we know something they don't know. All scholars sooner or later come to be like the daughters of the Hesperides in Tennyson:

> Out of watchings, out of wiles,
> Comes the bliss of secret smiles,
> All things are not told to all.

Hence, as time goes on, we need more groups for fewer members, and the solid compartments in knowledge that seemed to be established by language and historical periods begin to dissolve as synchronic, comparative and theoretical aspects of literature develop. Then again, in the last few years, the old simple image at the heart of humane studies, of somebody reading a book, has become as complex as a Duchamp painting. The reader is a conventionalized poetic fiction; the act of reading is the art of reading something else; the history of literature records only the pangs of misprized texts. The current programme suggests a Darwinian throwing out of variations at random until something adapts to a new environment. The possibility that the new environment is not there is one that we simply have to risk.

By a curious irony, the catholicity of the MLA creates a difficulty for its own periodical. Most learned journals are much narrower in range, and those who consult them know in advance the kind of thing they are looking for. In having to reflect the whole MLA conspectus, *PMLA*, according to many opinions I have heard, tends to become something of what Marshall McLuhan would call a cool medium of low definition, a collection of prize essays rather than a journal with a specific shape. But it would, in my opinion, be a mistake to undervalue the attempt to reflect the scholarship in the modern languages as a total community, however large and miscellaneous.

Another feature of the advance of knowledge takes longer to manifest itself. As a greater variety of people come to study the modern languages, it becomes clear that there is much in every past culture which is profoundly alienating. Our cultural traditions, as usually interpreted, are too male-centered for women, too white-centered for blacks, too *rentier*-centered for radicals, too heterosexual for the gay, too withdrawn for the engaged, too religious for the secular, too secular for the religious. We sometimes assume a large central majority, say a male white middle-class establishment, which is satisfied with the traditional emphases in culture, and anxious to resist changes in them. But there is no such majority, and there never really has been. Everybody's sympathies with the past are highly qualified: everybody has to make very selective efforts to make a personal contact with the chosen part of one's cultural heritage, and more means for expressing one's deeper personal interests have constantly to be provided. As most of the relevant documents, for these interests, are quite recent, we find ourselves swung over to the contemporary context of literary response.

The founders of the MLA felt that Greek and Latin had no monopoly on "classics"; but starting the title of the association with the word "modern" soon broke down the isolation of the classic from the contemporary. Besides, just as the Classics had had to face a competition with the modern languages that forced them into a minority place in the university, so the modern languages have had to face a similar competition with the social sciences. A glance at more recent programmes shows many discussion groups, ranging from language theory to what are politely called gyno-centric serial dramas, that reflect an interest very difficult, and quite unnecessary, to distinguish from the interest of a social science. The growing awareness of our sources of revenue, inside and outside the university, has the same effect. Whether the market is students or legislatures, the past does not sell like the present: sometimes it will not sell at all except in some present package like the "national interest".

The contemporary perspective reached a crisis about ten years ago, when we began to hear very different views about the university's place in society. The old conception of the university as a counter-environment is, we were told, quite illusory. A social system maintains the university for what it gets out of it, and what our system gets out of the humanities is an ideology that translates the facts of oligarchy into pseudo-democratic platitudes. The rationale of teaching is not to give students detachment, but to condition them to being kept off the labor market and out of the area of social decision. As for the scholarly attitude of mind, the belief that a certain kind of training will magically produce a certain kind of mentality simply ascribes to education what really belongs to social status.

The older humanist philosophy did distinguish knowledge and wisdom, but it assumed that knowledge was the only possible road to wisdom. Knowledge for it was knowledge of the actual: wisdom was rather a sense of the potential, the ability to adapt to a variety of situations which is developed out of knowledge. But, as I said, knowledge is secret and élitist by its very nature: what it really leads to is a mysterious expertise; and this, so far from broadening the social perspective, tends to narrow it. Such a narrowing, many people began to say, is at best pedantry, at worst an indifference to the real issues of our time, issues involving not only the well-being but even the continued existence of the human race, that verges on the psychotic. There has always been a different conception of wisdom, the conception preserved in the popular proverbs and fables which from ancient times have been among the few really democratic literary genres. This wisdom consists in the possession, by the community as a whole, of the essential axioms for sanity and survival. By ignoring or undervaluing this common wisdom in favor of expertise, education becomes a pernicious form of mass hypnosis.

We have heard some of this attitude in earlier presidential addresses to the MLA. I do not question the truth in it, certainly not the good faith of those who expounded it. But the movement it spoke for stopped short of an effective attack on the universities, and for a very good reason. Even among those most deeply dissatisfied with a capitalist-controlled democracy, relatively few regarded any other society, such as the Soviet Union, as providing a model for the transformation of those nearer home. And as the movement had no external model, so it had no clearly defined enemy: the real model and enemy were in ourselves. In this situation the old view of the university as a counter-environment, a place where criticism and dissent could be protected by various devices like tenure appointments, had to survive, if only *faute de mieux*. The sociology departments of the seventies are now well-stocked with student activists of the sixties. And as the university continued to hold its own, a new generation of students grew up in reaction to the preceding one, as new generations are so apt to do. I don't know what Pamela thought of her name when she got older, but there was once a critical magazine in Canada called *The Rebel*, and a couple connected with it named their daughter Rebel. When Rebel reached the age of seventeen she changed her name to Joy.

It would be easy to take a complacent attitude to the relative quiet of today, and say that the pendulum has swung back. It has, but we should look at the whole metaphor: when a pendulum swings back it is always later in time. Besides, if a radical reaction includes a good deal of hysteria, a conservative one is bound to include a good deal of inertia. The educational bureaucracy, after being prodded out of its massive incompetence for a few years after Sputnik, has now relapsed to what it considers normal, and the modern languages have suffered accordingly. The educational budget, like the defence budget on a small scale, is crushingly heavy and mostly wasted, and this naturally means a squeeze on the universities. The MLA is a place that people go to partly to give and get jobs: there are enough jokes about the slave market, and enough demonology about the department chairman who sits in his hotel room over a bottle and breaks down the morale of one applicant after another. But there is something in the MLA's continued concern for employment which is both realistic and humane. It is still doing what it can, but it is crippled by a budget squeeze too, and there is not much it can do if the situation is aggravated by a decline in the solidarity of the profession itself.

By solidarity in the profession I naturally do not mean advancing people regardless of their merits, nor am I convinced that unions are the answer, or the permanent answer. For one thing, there is a difficulty in finding the boundary line between labor and management. Like other older academics, I spend a lot of time writing letters of recommendation for jobs, promotions and tenure appointments, and I get a strong impression that not only the administration but the senior teaching staff in many universities will snatch at almost any excuse to deny these things. By solidarity I mean the sense that no scholar is an island: everyone's scholarly fortunes are inseparable from those of one's colleagues and of the profession as a whole. Students emerging from graduate school with a genuine vocation and commitment are a part of my own scholarly life, and their frustrations and humiliations frustrate and humiliate me also. This clearly points either to stomach ulcers or to some attempt at organized professional action. I have no programme of my own for such action — it too would have to be a complex and co-operative enterprise — but I would not despair of the possibility.

By 1976, the MLA heard an eloquent plea for solidarity from Professor Germaine Brée, in which she soberly reminded us that there is no substitute for the first essential thing, a belief in our own subject and in its importance for society. She quoted Ronald Berman of the NEH as saying that what was needed was not so much money as a body of intellectual conviction, and she added:

> This does not seem to be in plentiful supply among us. Not, I think, out of a basic indifference, but because we have no estab-

lished curriculum in relation to which we can define our place
and usefulness as an academic discipline.

I should like to comment briefly on this text in conclusion.

Certainly, students come to us knowing far less than they
should: it is quite possible to design a school curriculum that
would waste less of their time and of ours, and there can be no
giving up the fight for better standards. But the situation will not
change overnight, and even if it did, it is also possible to get
trapped by metaphors of progress and steady advance. We may feel
that if students reached university properly baked in their various
age-layers, we could add an impressive architectural icing. But
there is always a great deal of unlearning and beginning again at
every stage of education. We find in our own experience that the
feeling of progressive advance is very rare, and that scholarship is
mostly a matter of continuous fumbling for a light switch in a dark
room. It is hardly reasonable to expect more from students.

In any case no teacher thinks of himself as stuffing information into young people who haven't got any. Students have
acquired a large body of verbal experience, of which perhaps one
per cent has been derived from anything recognizable as literature.
We have the whole of this experience to deal with, not merely the
one per cent, and have to be guided by broader principles than
information. One of these is the principle of freedom which is
inherent in the whole conception of a liberal education. Literacy,
the primary act of learning to read, sets one free to take part in a
modern industrial society. But every society is set up in such a way
that what one primarily learns to read are things like advertise-
ments and traffic signs, that is, directions or exhortations to
conform. The real freedom lies behind, the freedom that comes
only from articulateness, the ability to produce as well as respond
to verbal structures.

Trying to liberate students by increasing their power to
articulate is a militant activity, carried on in the teeth of inertia,
confusion and ignorance. Each of us has to relearn in the classroom the lesson that Milton learned from the Civil War: that
freedom is something people say they want but don't really want.
Genuine freedom and discipline are the same thing: one cannot be
set free to play the piano or speak German without a long period of
directed attention and practice. But for most people freedom
means only what Arnold called doing as one likes, that is, getting

pushed around by one's inner compulsions. In adolescence particularly there are strong pressures toward introversion on the one hand, and rigid conformity to group action on the other. Both of these, as we saw in the hippie movement of a few years ago, tend to make a fetish of inarticulateness.

With the awareness of freedom comes the awareness that language is much more than simply an area of knowledge. Everything we know is formed out of words and numbers, and literature and mathematics are the only subjects of knowledge which are also means of knowing. A student in Toronto recently attached a note to his political science essay reading: "Please do not take marks off for grammar or style, because I am not and have never claimed to be an English scholar". The confusion resulting from thinking of the languages purely as bodies of knowledge like other bodies of knowledge could hardly go further. Such a student has still to learn that what we express badly we do not know: we have only the illusion of knowing it.

Teachers are ranked by society in an unofficial hierarchy according to the age of their students, and the university teacher is thought of as further up in the hierarchy than the grade two teacher, even though it is clear that the more elementary the level of teaching, the more important it is that it be done properly. It is perhaps a similar perversion of values that ranks the languages rather low in the university itself: they are low in budget and administrative esteem, low in the sense of being where the action is. I think that the instrumental quality of language teaching has much to do with this: the fact that a student must learn words before any other kind of learning is of any use to him, must be articulate before he can be a real person, must know more than his native language to live with any awareness in a world like ours. It may be right to think of ourselves as service departments, like the maintenance staff, but we should also sometimes think of how much depends on us, and of how important it is to keep on fighting for the only kind of social change that makes any real or lasting sense. As for our scholarship and research, what sustained me, as it still does, when I first went into the study of literature, was the feeling that I had the best subject-matter in the world, and a job to do with it that literature could not do by itself. It distresses me that literary scholars still tease themselves with the notion of criticism as failed creation, and continue to explain to one another, in a kind of ecstasy of masochism, how vain, futile and parasitic the critical enterprise really is.

For some time now I have been interested in the relation of the Bible to European literature. It is the sort of topic that, whenever one gets at all close to it, sends one back again with a sense of the total irrelevance of everything one knows, or thinks one knows. Yet the suggestion in it of infinite mysteries connected with *logos* or articulate speech is as fascinating to the literary critic in me as a flame to a moth, even if in the end it proves equally destructive. There are two conceptions in particular involved in the study of the Bible that I am still nowhere near really understanding: they are wisdom, already referred to, and prophecy.

Both words clearly have different levels in their biblical contexts. The primitive meaning of wisdom seems to be following the tried and tested way; its chief form of expression is the proverb, the counsel of prudence that keeps our balance in life from one day to the next; its opposite is the fool with his new idea that always turns out to be an old fallacy. Such wisdom goes with conservatism, the authority of seniors, the acceptance of a fixed framework of education, and the anxiety of continuity, of getting through life without being confronted by a dialectical choice. Prophecy seems to start from the opposite direction: the primitive prophets were mediums or oracles who could go into a trance and speak with a different voice, interpreted as the voice of the local god. And just as wisdom is conservative, continuous, and linked to the past, so prophecy is discontinuous, radical, and linked to the future. The prophet does not accept established society, but repudiates it, along with all its wisdom, in the name of a deity who has higher standards, and the focus of his prophecy is a final transcending of the social order.

But as the two conceptions develop they get less unlike. The prophet becomes less of an ecstatic and more of an adviser or counsellor, and the wise man comes to be thought of as having a potential of utterance called forth by certain occasions. Both are drawn towards the present, and away from the past and future. And as wisdom and prophecy approach each other, it becomes clear that there is a point where they meet and become the same thing, the point where there is no longer any wise man or any prophet, but simply the word itself, a power of speech articulating itself independently of the speaker's ego. Perhaps this is the point described by Heidegger in his later essays, where he calls language the master and not the servant of man, and tells us that it is really language that speaks, man speaking only through a response to language.

Scholars are temperamentally disposed to be conservative and protected by institutions: creative people often have ecstatic or other involuntary powers, and are apt to be free-wheeling in their social attitudes and unreasonably radical or reactionary in their political views. Scholars and creative writers seem to have many psychological links with the wise men and prophets respectively of earlier times. In the study of language and literature the scholarly aspect of the human mind is struggling with the creative aspect. Each is also involved in its own struggle. The scholar is concerned with the continuous accumulation of knowledge, yet all the time there is an underlying drive toward a more discontinuous kind of wisdom, an insight for which all knowledge is only a symbol and literature itself only a means. The writer is concerned with becoming a distinctive creative voice in literature, yet in him there is again a drive toward some kind of 'zero degree of writing', as it has been called, where the literary and all its conventions disappear and only the pure prophetic vision is left.

Our real reasons for doing something are usually different from our formulated ones: perhaps the real motivation in literary scholarship is a sense that literature is not a territory to be conquered by critics who divide it up according to the chance of perference, but a common cause that unites all of us with all of it. Such a motivation could exist only if there were, ultimately, some sense behind it of an identity of criticism and creation, of scholarship and teaching, of the search for knowledge and the production of vision, an identity produced by the authority of the word speaking for itself. The awareness of this identity may be unconscious, but then some critics have suggested that the unconscious itself is linguistically structured. If the awareness ever rose directly into our consciousness, as a full vision of the role of words in human life, I suspect that it would become something very close to what in times past has been symbolized by the gift of tongues.

Humanities in a New World

In his satirical romance *Erewhon*, published in 1872, Samuel Butler describes the "Colleges of Unreason," which taught mainly the "hypothetical languages," languages of great difficulty that never existed. The professors were obsessed with the notion that in this world all well-bred people must compromise, hence they instructed their students never to commit themselves on any point. They had professorships of Inconsistency and Evasion, and students were plucked in examinations for a lack of vagueness in their answers. There was however a more modern feeling that examinations should be abolished altogether, the competition involved being regarded as "self-seeking and unneighborly." The strictest of the professors was the professor of Worldly Wisdom, who was also President of the Society for the Suppression of Useless Knowledge, and for the Completer Obliteration of the Past. Butler concludes that at these Colleges "The art of sitting gracefully on a fence has never, I should think, been brought to greater perfection."

The point of Butler's satire is that the more the university tries to remain aloof from society, the more slavishly it will follow the accepted patterns of that society. The tendencies that Butler ridicules are those of a social system in which the ideal is a gentle-manly amateur, with no definite occupation. The university that confronts us today still reflects accepted social attitudes, but those attitudes have changed, and the university has changed with them. The university is now well aware of its social function, and if it were not, public opinion would compel it to become so. Professors are still unwilling to commit themselves, but their reasons are no longer abstract social reasons, but concrete political ones.

Above all, the ideal of productivity, the vision of the unob-structed assembly line, has taken over the university as it has every-thing else. The professor today is less a learned man than a "productive scholar." He is trained in graduate school to become productive by an ingenious but simple device. It is a common academic failing to dream of writing the perfect book, and then, because no achievement can reach perfection, not writing it. One of the major scholarly enterprises on the University of Toronto campus, Professor Kathleen Coburn's edition of the note-books of Coleridge, is the result of the fact that Coleridge never wrote his gigantic masterpiece, the treatise on the Logos that would tell the world what Coleridge knew, but hugged it to his bosom in the form of fifty-seven note-books. *Nous avons changé tout cela.* Our graduate student today must finish a thesis, a document which is, practically by definition, something that nobody particularly wants either to write or to read. This teaches him that it is more important to produce than to perfect, and that it is less anti-social to contribute to knowledge than to possess it.

In Butler's day there were no PhD's in English, but since then there has been a vast increase in the systematizing of scholarship. The modern library, with its stacks and microfilms; modern recordings, reproductions of pictures, aids in learning languages: all these are part of a technological revolution that has trans-formed the humanities equally with the sciences. There were Canadian poets and novelists a century ago, and critics who reviewed and discussed their work, but there was not the same sense of the systematic processing of the literature that there is now. Of course, wherever there is a cult of productivity there is a good deal of hysteria. New students come along with reputations to make; new poets arise to be commented on; learned journals multiply and their subsidies divide; bibliographies lengthen, and so does the list of works that a scholar feels apologetic about not having read. There seems no answer to this steadily increasing strain on the scholarly economy except the Detroit answer, that next year's books will be still bigger, duller, fuller of superfluous detail, and more difficult to house. If I were speaking only to scholars in the humanities, I should say merely that this is our business, and that we can take care of it. But as I am speaking to a wider public, I should like also to try to explain, if I can, what difference our business makes in the world.

I begin with the fact that the faculty of arts and sciences, or more briefly the faculty of arts, seems to be the centre of the University. A big modern university could almost be defined as whatever group of professional schools in one town happens to be held together by a faculty of arts. We can have a university that is nothing but a faculty of arts; on the other hand, a professional school, set up by itself, is not a university, although it may resemble university life in many ways.

The reason for this is not hard to see as far as science is concerned. The university is the powerhouse of civilization, and the centre of the university has to correspond to the actual centres of human knowledge. Engineering is practical or applied science; medicine is really another form of applied science. And if we ask what it is that gets applied in these professions, the answer is clearly science, as conceived and studied in the faculty of arts. The basis of technology, or applied science, is a disinterested research, carried on without regard to its practical applications, ready to take the risk of being thought useless or socially indifferent or morally neutral, concerned only with developing the science, not with improving the lot of mankind. Technology by itself cannot produce the kind of scientist that it needs for its own development: at any rate, that seems to be the general opinion of those who are qualified to have an opinion on the subject.

Attached to the sciences are what we call the liberal arts or humanities. What are they doing at the centre of university life? Are they there because they must be there, or merely because they have always been there? Are they functional in the modern world, or only ornamental? The simplest way to answer these questions is to go back to the principle on which, in the Middle Ages, the seven liberal arts were divided into two groups. The two great instruments that man has devised for understanding and transforming the world are words and numbers. The humanities are primarily the *verbal* disciplines; the natural sciences are the numerical ones.

The natural sciences are concerned very largely with measurement, and at their centre is mathematics, the disinterested study of numbers, or quantitative relationships. At the centre of the humanities, corresponding to mathematics, is language and literature, the disinterested study of words, a study which ranges from phonetics to poetry. Around it, corresponding to the natural sciences, are history and philosophy, which are concerned with the verbal organization of events and ideas.

And just as we have engineering and other forms of applied science, so there is a vast area of what we may call verbal technology, the use of words for practical or useful purposes. The two words practical and useful do not of course mean quite the same thing: some forms of verbal technology, like preaching, may be useful without always being practical; others, like advertising, may be practical without always being useful. Many of the university's professional schools — law, theology, education — are concerned with verbal technology, and so is every area of human knowledge that employs words as well as numbers, metaphors as well as equations, definition as well as measurement. A century ago the central subjects in arts were Classics and mathematics, Classics being restricted to Greek and Latin. Today the central subjects are still Classics and mathematics, but Classics has broadened out to take in all the languages in óur cultural orbit, beginning with our own.

This seems clear enough: why are people so confused about the humanities, and more especially confused about literature? There are many answers, but the important one is quite simple. A student who learns only a few pages of Latin grammar will never see the point of having learned even that; and today he learns so little English in early life that the majority of our young people can hardly be said to possess even a native language. "I think," said Sir Philip Sidney, "(it) was a piece of the Tower of Babylon's curse, that a man should be put to school to learn his mother tongue." But it is no use pretending that the curse of Babel does not exist. Behind *Paradise Lost*, behind *Hamlet*, behind *The Faerie Queene*, lay years of daily practice in translating Latin into English, English into Latin, endless themes written and corrected and rewritten, endless copying and imitation of the Classical writers, endless working and reworking of long lists of rhetorical devices with immense Greek names. Discipline of this kind is apparently impossible in the modern school, where teachers are not only overworked but subjected to anti-literary pressures. They are encouraged, sometimes compelled, to substitute various kinds of slick verbal trash for literature; they are bedevilled with audio-visual and other aids to distraction; their curricula are prescribed by a civil service which in its turn responds to pressure from superstitious or prurient voters. In the verbal arts, the student of eighteen is about where he should be at fourteen, apart from what he does on his own with the help of a sympathetic teacher or librarian. To say this is not to reflect on the schools, but on the social conditions that cripple them.

So the student often enters college with the notion that reading and writing are elementary subjects that he mastered in childhood. He may never clearly have grasped the fact that there are differences in levels of reading and writing, as there are in mathematics between short division and integral calculus. He is disconcerted to find that, after thirteen years of schooling, he is still, by any civilized standard, illiterate. Further, that a lifetime of study will never bring him to the point at which he has read enough or can write well enough. Still, he is, let us say, an intelligent and interested student with a reasonable amount of good will — most students are, fortunately. He begins to try to write essays, perhaps without ever having written five hundred consecutive words in his life before, and the first results take the form of that verbal muddle which is best called jargon. He is now on the lowest rung of the literary ladder, on a level with the distributors of gobbledygook, double talk and officialese of all kinds; of propaganda, public relations and Timestyle; of the education textbook that is not lucky enough to be rewritten in the publisher's office.

By jargon I do not mean the use of technical terms in a technical subject. Technical language may make one's prose look bristly and forbidding, but if the subject is genuinely specialized there is no way to get out of using it. By jargon I mean writing in which words do not express meanings, but are merely thrown in the general direction of their meanings; writing which can always be cut down by two-thirds without loss of whatever sense it has. Jargon always unconsciously reveals a personal attitude. There is the blustering jargon that says to the reader, "Well, anyway, you know what I mean." Such writing exhibits a kind of squalid arrogance, roughly comparable to placing a spittoon on the opposite side of the room. There is the coy jargon which, like the man with one talent, wants to wrap up and hide away what it says so that no reader will be able to dig it. There is the dithering jargon that is afraid of the period, and jerks along in a series of dashes, a relay race whose torch has long since gone out. There is the morally debased jargon of an easily recognized type of propaganda, with its greasy clotted abstractions, its weaseling arguments, and its undertone of menace and abuse. There is the pretentious jargon of those who feel that anything readable must be unscientific. And finally, there is the jargon produced by our poor student, which is often the result simply of a desire to please. If he were studying journalism, he would imitate the jargon of journalism; as he is being asked to write by professors, he produces the kind of verbal cotton-wool which is his idea of the way professors write. What is worse, it is the way that a lot of them do write.

When teachers of the humanities attack and ridicule jargon, they do not do so merely because it offends their aesthetic sensibilities, offensive as it is in that respect. They attack it because they understand the importance of a professional use of words. The natural sciences, we said, are largely concerned with measurement, which means accurate measurement. In any subject that uses words, the words have to be used with precision, clarity and power, otherwise the statements made in them will be either meaningless or untrue. Lawyers, for example, use words in a way very different from the poets, but their use of them is precise in their field, as anyone who tries to draft a law without any legal training will soon discover. And what is true of law cannot be less true of sociology or metaphysics or literary criticism.

It is often thought that teachers of the humanities judge everything in words by a pedantic and rather frivolous standard of correctness. They don't care, it is felt, what one really means; all they care about is whether one says "between you and I," or uses "contact" and "proposition" as verbs. Now it is true that the humanities are based on the accepted forms of grammar, spelling, pronunciation, syntax and meaning. If a man says he will pay you what he owes you next Toisday, it is useful to know whether he means Tuesday or Thursday: if there were no accepted forms there could be no communication. Teachers in the humanities are also concerned with preventing words from being confused with other words, with preserving useful distinctions among words, with trying to make the methods of good writers in the past available for writers today, with trying to steer a civilized course between dictionary dictatorship and mob rule. Some snobbery is bound to be attached to the ability to use words correctly. We hear a good deal about that.

For some reason we hear less about the much greater amount of snob appeal in vulgarity. Most of the people who say "throwed" instead of "threw" know well enough that "threw" is the accepted form, but are not going to be caught talking good grammar. On other social levels there is a feeling that the natural destiny of those who can handle words properly is to form a kind of genteel servant class: ghost writers who turn out books and speeches for the unlettered great; secretaries who translate the gargles and splutters of their bosses into letters written in English; preachers and professors and speakers at clubs who function as middle-class entertainers. Such a conception of society is very like that of a P.G. Wodehouse novel, where the butler speaks in a formal nineteenth-century style and his wealthy young master talks like a mentally retarded child. Then again, as Henry James pointed out fifty years ago in his book *The American Scene*, there was a time when the absorption of the North American male in business led to the domination of all the rest of civilized life by the woman. The result has been that the word culture, which strictly means everything that man has accomplished since he came down out of the trees, has come to acquire a strongly feminine cast. This sense of the word survives in the silly clichés that people use to prevent themselves from thinking, such as "longhair," or, most fatuous and slovenly of them all, "ivory tower," a phrase which has become popular because it sounds vaguely female and sexual, like a calendar girl in *Esquire*. But this male absorption in business was the product of an expanding economy and weak labour unions: it is now drawing to a close, and in matters of culture the woman is being joined by what Henry James, with his usual delicacy, called her sleeping partner.

Our student, with a little practice, will soon advance from jargon to the beginnings of prose, which means advancing from an amateurish to a professional approach to words. To make such an advance involves an important moral and psychological change. Bad writers are like bad car-drivers: what they are doing is the unconscious expression of a way of life. The purveyors of jargon are like the man who honks and hustles his way through traffic to advertise the importance of his business, or the woman who wants to hit something in order to prove that she is helpless and appealing. The good car-driver regards his or her activity as a simple but highly specific skill, unconnected with the rest of the personality. The good writer is the writer who puts self-expression aside, and is ready to submit himself to the discipline of words.

In the past, and under the influence of the old faculty psychology, the different fields of study were correlated with different parts of the mind. Thus history was ascribed to the memory, poetry to the imagination, and philosophy and science to the reason. This way of thinking has left many traces in our day: it is still widely believed that a mathematician is an unemotional reasoner, and a poet a "genius," a word which usually means emotionally unbalanced. But, of course, any difficult study demands the whole mind, not pieces of it. Reason and a sense of fact are as important to the novelist as they are to the chemist; genius and creative imagination play the same role in mathematics that they do in poetry. A similar fallacy may be confusing our student at this critical point. I am, he perhaps feels, a conscious being; I know I can think; I know I have ideas that are waiting to be put into words. I wish somebody would show me how to express my ideas, instead of shoving all this poetry stuff at me. After all, poets put their *feelings* into words, so they can make sounds and pictures out of them; but that isn't what I want.

Every step in this chain of reasoning is wrong, so it is no wonder if the reasoner is confused. In the first place, thinking is not a natural process like eating or sleeping. The difficulty here is partly semantic: we are apt to speak of all our mental processes as forms of thought. Musing, day-dreaming, associating, remembering, worrying: every slop and gurgle of our mental sewers we call thinking. If we are asked a question and can only guess at the answer, we begin with the words "I think." But real thinking is an acquired skill founded on practice and habit, like playing the piano, and how well we can think at any given time will depend on how much of it we have already done. Nor can we think at random: we can only add one more idea to the body of something we have already thought about. In fact we, as individuals or egos, can hardly be said to think at all: we link our minds to an objective body of thought, follow its facts and processes, and finally, if the links are strong enough, our minds become a place where something new in the body of thought comes to light.

It is the same with the imaginative thinking of literature. The great writer seldom regards himself as a personality with something to say: his mind to him is simply a place where something happens to words. T.S. Eliot compares the poet to a catalyzer, which accompanies but does not bring about the process it is used for; Keats speaks of the poet's negative capability; Wordsworth of his recollection in tranquility; Milton of the dictation of unpremeditated verse by a Muse. The place where the greatest fusions of words have occurred in English was in the mind of Shakespeare, and Shakespeare, as a personality, was so self-effacing that he has irritated some people into a frenzy of trying to prove that he never existed.

If the student were studying natural science, he would grasp this principle of objective thought very quickly. There can be no self-expressive approach to physics or chemistry: one has to learn the laws of the science first before one can have anything to express in it. But the same thing is true of the verbal disciplines. The student is not really struggling with his own ideas, but with the laws and principles of words. In any process of genuine thought that involves words, there can be no such thing as an inarticulate idea waiting to have words put around it. The words are the forms of which the ideas are the content, and until the words have been found, the idea does not exist.

A student of engineering may have extremely practical aims in entering that field, but he cannot get far without mathematics. Hence mathematics, though not in itself a practical subject, is practical enough for him. For a student who is going to engage in any verbal activity, the study of literature, not in itself a practical subject, is a practical necessity. The sciences deal with facts and truths, but mathematics sets one free from the particular case: it leads us from three apples to three, and from a square field to a square. Literature has the same function in the humanities. The historian is concerned with finding the right words for the facts; the philosopher, with finding the right words for the truth. As compared with the historian, the poet is concerned, Aristotle tells us, not with what happened but with the kind of thing that does happen. As compared with the philosopher, the poet is concerned, not with specific statements, but with the images, metaphors, symbols and verbal patterns out of which all directed thinking comes. Mathematics is useful, but pure mathematics, apart from its use, is one of the major disciplines of beauty. Poetry, is, in itself, beautiful, but if we think of it as merely decorative or emotional, that is because we have not learned to use it. We can build the most gigantic structures out of words and numbers, but we have constantly to return to literature and mathematics, because they show us the infinite possibilities that there are in words and numbers themselves. Sir James Jeans, speaking of the failure of nineteenth-century physics to build a mechanical model of the universe, says that the Supreme Architect of the universe must be a mathematician. A much older authority informs us that the Supreme Teacher of mankind was a story-teller, who never taught without a parable.

The humanities in the university are supposed to be concerned with criticism and scholarship, not with creation as such. At the centre of literature lie the "classics," the works that university teachers know they can respect, and the university student, *qua* student, is there to study them, not to write on his own. True, most writers of importance today are not only university graduates but university employees, at least in summer sessions. True, the untaught writer who sends a masterpiece to a publisher from out of nowhere is much more a figure of folklore than of actual literature. Still, the university does not try to foster the social conditions under which great literature can be produced. In the first place, we do not know what these conditions are; in the second place, we have no reason to suppose that they are good conditions. Just as doctors are busiest in an epidemic, so our dramatists and novelists may find their best subjects where decadence, brutality, or idiocy show human behaviour in its more fundamental patterns. Or the producer of literature himself may be a drunk, a homosexual, a Fascist, a philanderer; in short, he may want things that the university cannot guarantee to supply.

The university, therefore, addresses itself to the consumer of literature, not to the producer. The consumer of literature is the cultivated man, the man of liberal education and disciplined taste, for whose benefit the poet has worked, suffered, despaired, or even wrecked his life. What the university does try to do is to foster the social conditions under which literature can be appreciated. Many teachers of the humanities are anxious to stop at that point, especially those who wish that they have been great poets instead. It is natural for them to insist that critics and scholars have no real function except to brush off the poet's hat and hand it to him. But a merely passive appreciation of literature is not enough. As Gerard Manley Hopkins said: "The effect of studying masterpieces is to make me admire and do otherwise." He was a poet, but he has exactly defined, even for non-poets, the effect of great writing, which is great because it is infinitely suggestive, and encourages us not to imitate it, but to do what we can in our own way. To appreciate literature is also to use it, to absorb it into our own lives and activities. There is unlikely to be much of a gap between what the humanities will do in a new world and what they are trying to do in this one. Teachers of the humanities understand the importance of what they are doing, and in any new world worth living in, nine-tenths of their effort would be to go on doing it. Still, I think they will become increasingly interested in the ways in which words and verbal patterns do affect human lives. They are likely to follow the direction indicated by the poet Wallace Stevens in one of his long discursive poems:

> This endlessly elaborating poem
> Displays the theory of poetry
> As the life of poetry. A more severe,
>
> More harassing master would extemporize
> Subtler, more urgent proof that the theory
> Of poetry is the theory of life.

A few years ago there was a great vogue for something called "semantics," which purported to be, not simply a certain type of literary study, but a panacea for human ills. People get neurotic, we were told, by attaching private and emotional significances to words: once they learn to use words properly, to bring them into alignment with the world around them, their psychological distresses and tensions will clear up. A minor advantage would be the abolishing of literature, where words are so thickly coated with emotional associations. Like other miraculous cures, semantics of this type achieved a great success among the hysterical, but failed to do everything it promised to do. It looks as though, as long as men are discussing matters that affect their pocketbooks, their homes or their lives, they will continue to attach emotional significance to the words they use. Perhaps it would be better to recognize that there is no short cut to verbal accuracy, and go back to study the poets, who have not tried to get rid of emotion, but have tried to make it precise. Nevertheless, the semanticists were right about the importance of words in human life, about the immediacy and intimacy of their impact, about their vast powers for good or for evil.

We use words in two ways: to make statements and arguments and convey information, or what passes as such, and to appeal to the imagination. The former is the province of history, philosophy and the social sciences; the latter is the province of literature. There is also a large intermediate area of what is called rhetoric, the art of verbal persuasion, where both means are employed. We are brought up to believe that words stand for things, and that most of our experience with words takes the form of reported fact, argument, and logical inference. This is a flattering self-delusion. Most of our daily experience with words takes place on a low level of the imagination — that is, it is sub-literary. I am writing this on the subway, and my eye falls on an advertisement for heavy-duty floor wax. Nothing could be more honestly factual; but even here "heavy duty" is a metaphor, probably of military origin, and the metaphor, with its imaginative overtones of ruggedness, strength and endurance, is the focus of the sales appeal. If the advertiser has something expensive or useless to sell, this sub-literary appeal is stepped up. One cannot read far in advertising without encountering over-writing, a too earnestly didactic tone, an uncritical acceptance of snobbish standards, and obtrusive sexual symbolism. These are precisely the qualities of inferior literature.

Then there are the other sub-literary areas of soap operas, movies, magazine stories, jokes, comic strips, gossip. It is out of the steady rain of imaginative impressions from these and similar quarters that most people form their myths: that is, their notions of representative human situations, of typical human characters and characteristics, of what is inspiring and what is ridiculous, of the socially acceptable and the socially outcast. It is here that the kind of preferences develop which determine one to condemn or condone segregation, to support or decry the United Nations, to vote for Mr. Diefenbaker or for Mr. Pearson. For even election issues and current events reach us chiefly through human-interest stories and personal impressions. For better or worse, it is through his literary imagination, such as it is, that modern man participates in society.

The responsible citizen, of course, tries to get away from mythical stereotypes, to read better papers and seek out friends who have some respect for facts and for rational discussion. But he will never succeed in raising his standards unless he educates his imagination too, for nothing can drive bad literature out of the mind except good literature. In these days we have an exaggerated sense of the power of argument and indoctrination. "Ideas are weapons" was a once fashionable phrase, and during the war publishers carried the slogan "books are weapons in the war of ideas." But arguments and aggressive ideas have a very limited role to play in human life. They that take the argument will perish by the argument; any statement that can be argued about at all can be refuted. The natural response to indoctrination is resistance, and nothing will make it successful except a well organized secret police. What can never be refuted is the underlying vision of life which all such arguments try to rationalize. The arguments are based on assumptions about what is worth living for or dying for; these are rooted in the imagination, and only the imagination can nourish them.

The distinction that we have made between the disciplines of words and numbers does not quite correspond to the distinction between the arts and the sciences. There are arts that do not depend on words, like music and painting, and there are sciences that do, like the social sciences. The real difference between art and science is expressed by Francis Bacon in *The Advancement of Learning:*

> The use of (poetry) hath been to give some shadow of satisfaction to the mind of Man in those points where the Nature of things doth deny it, the world being in proportion inferior to the soul . . . And therefore (poetry) was ever thought to have some participation of divineness, because it doth raise and erect the Mind, by submitting the shews of things to the desires of the Mind, whereas reason doth buckle and bow the Mind unto the Nature of things.

The sciences, in other words, are primarily concerned with the world as it is: the arts are primarily concerned with the world that man wants to live in. The sciences have among other things the function of showing man how much he can realize of what he wants to do, and how much has to remain on the level of wish or fantasy. In between comes the area of applied science and applied art, where the process of realization is accomplished. Architecture is one obvious place in which science and art meet on a practical basis. Art, then, owes its existence to man's dissatisfaction with nature and his desire to transform the physical world into a human one. Religion itself, when it deals with ultimate things, uses the language of art, and speaks of an eternal city and a restored garden as the fulfilling of the soul's desires. The human imagination, which the arts address, is not an escape from reality, but a vision of the world in its human form.

Science continually evolves and improves: the scientist contributes to an expanding body of knowledge, and the freshman studying physics today can sit on the shoulders of Newton and Faraday, knowing things that they did not know. The arts, on the other hand, produce the classic or model, which may be equalled by something different, but is never improved on. The greatest artists have reached the limits of what their art can do: there is an infinite number of limits to be reached, and artists of the future will reach many of them, but it makes nonsense of the conception of art to think of it as developing. The painters in the stone age caverns were as highly developed as Picasso; Homer is as much a model for poets today as he was for Virgil. We have as great art as humanity can ever produce with us now. The natural direction of science, then, is onward: it moves toward still greater achievements in the future. The arts have this in common with religion, that their direction is not onward into the future but upward from where we stand.

The point of contact between the arts and the human mind is the moment of leisure, one of the most misunderstood words in the language. Leisure is not idleness, which is neurotic, and still less is it distraction, which is psychotic. Leisure begins in that moment of consciousness peculiar to a rational being, when we become aware of our own existence and can watch ourselves act, when we have time to think of the worth and purpose of what we are doing, to compare it with what we might or would rather be doing. It is the moment of the birth of human freedom, when we are able to subject what is actual to the standard of what is possible. William Blake calls it the moment in the day that Satan cannot find. It is a terrifying moment for many of us, like the opening of a Last Judgement in the soul, and our highways and television sets are crowded with people who are not seeking leisure but are running away from it. The same is true of the compulsive worker, the man who boasts of how little leisure he has, and who speeds himself up until he explodes in neuroses and stomach ulcers.

We tend to think of leisure as having nothing in particular to do: this is what the word means in Thorstein Veblen's *Theory of the Leisure Class*, where he is examining the traditional idea of the gentleman as the man who does not work. But even the old leisure class did possess some essential social values — courtesy, good taste, patronage of the arts — and a democracy has the problem of trying to retain those genuine values, while making them accessible to anyone. It is still true that liberal education is the education of the free man, and has no meaning out of the context of freedom. The really privileged person is not the man who has no work to do, but the man who works freely, and has voluntarily assumed his duties in the light of his conception of himself and his social function. The underprivileged person is (at best) the servile worker, or what Carlyle called the drudge, and every social advance, every technological invention, every improvement in labour relations, has the aim of reducing the amount of servile work in society. But what makes free work free is its relation to the vision of life that begins in the moment of leisure. The poet Yeats took as a motto for one of his books the phrase "in dreams begin responsibilities." It is also in man's dream of a humanized world that all learning, art and science begin. As Aristotle pointed out, the words school and scholarship come from *schole*, leisure. The Bible says that leisure is the beginning of wisdom, but the two statements are quite compatible, for religion too has its origin in leisure. Christianity illustrated this fact when it changed a day of rest at the end of the week into a day of leisure at the beginning of the week. The university illustrates the same principle, in its secular form, when it places a four-year voluntary liberal education at the beginning of adult life.

We also tend to think of the rewards of leisure as individual possessions, like the love of poetry or music that fills the spare intervals of our lives with private moments of grace and beauty. But behind these private possessions lies a social possession, a vision of life that we share with others. This shared vision is the total form of art, man's vision of a human world, to which every individual work of art belongs. Most of us are seldom aware of the power of words in forming the visions which hold society together. Special occasions, like the familiar words spoken at marriages and funerals, or a critical moment in history that we happen to live through, like the summer of 1940 when the free world had practically nothing but Churchill's prose style left to fight with, are usually all that bring them to our minds.

Yet any newspaper can show us how society turns on the hinges of words and numbers. The people who make fortunes out of uranium stocks owe their wealth and social prestige to an absent-minded professor, badly in need of a haircut, who scribbled down e=mc² on a piece of paper fifty years ago. The Republicans owe their existence to the fact that a century ago a long-legged Illinois lawyer put a few words together that made up a social vision for the American people of genuine dignity and power, and so enabled the Republican party to stand for something. Communism owes its existence to the fact that a century ago a carbuncular political agitator disappeared into the British Museum to write a sprawling, badly organized and grittily technical book on capitalism, which even its author was unable to finish. I have no doubt that the philosophy and economics of that work have been refuted many times, but no refutation will have any effect on it. Marxism is a vision of life, with its roots in the social imagination, and it will endure, at least as a vision, until another of greater intensity grows up in its place.

The people who run away from their own leisure will, of course, also run away from the articulate sounds of words that would recall them to their dreams and their responsibilities. Just as a frightened child may be reassured to hear the murmur of his parents' voices downstairs, so the childish in our society turn to the books and newspapers, the television programmes and the political leaders, that supply them with the endless, unmeaning babble of the lonely crowd. If you remember George Orwell's *1984*, you will recall the decisive role of "Newspeak" in that book. There is only one way to degrade mankind permanently, and that is to destroy language. The whole history of ordered public speech, from the Hebrew prophets who denounced their kings and the Demosthenes and Cicero who fought for the Classical republics down through Milton and Jefferson and Mill and Lincoln, has been inseparably a part of the heritage of freedom. In the nature of things — or rather in the nature of words — it cannot be otherwise. We naturally demand leadership from our leaders, but thugs and gangsters can give us leadership, of a kind: if we demand articulateness as well, we are demanding something that only a genuine vision of human life can provide.

The Writer
and the University

Universities in a democracy must remain universities, and that means academic freedom, the unrestricted pursuit of undiscovered truth, and not the repeating of the truths that the different pressure groups in society think they already have. All pressure groups in society are anti-educational, no matter what they are pressing for. In Wilkie Collins' detective story *The Moonstone* there's an unpleasant nosy female who speaks of "the blessed prospect of interfering," and there are people like that in every country. But the more remote and diverse the financial support of a university is, the less easy it is for them to get inspired by that prospect.

Now, with the Canada Council Act, federal aid for universities is linked with federal aid for culture. The principles involved for culture are precisely the same. Federal aid cannot be the sole or even the main financial support of Canadian culture, but having it establishes the same double recognition of its necessity and its freedom: it has to be there, and it has to be left alone. It is logical to link the university and culture: in fact it could almost be said that the university today is to culture what the church is to religion: the social institution that makes it possible. It teaches the culture of the past, and it tries to build up an educated public for the culture of the present.

In the Soviet Union, as I understand it, culture is regarded as a function of the state, and hence all culture comes directly under political criticism. I dare say a great deal of lively discussion results, which may often be quite free in its own context, or even help the artist from a Marxist point of view. Still, the principle involved strikes us here in the democracies as pernicious. Yet it seems to me that a good deal of public thinking about culture here is still stuck in the laissez-faire economics of a century ago. For us the writer is still a small retailer, who has to be subsidized to compete with the mass media. This makes the writer an economic absurdity. A few novelists, most of them bad ones, may eke out a small living by writing, or even hit a best-seller jackpot; but a poet would have to be spectacularly bad before he could live on his poetry. The writer, unlike the painter, has nothing to sell that becomes the exclusive property of the buyer. Speaking of literature, which is the aspect of culture I know most about, I should say that the writer as such really has no economic position at all, and depends for his living on various official and semi-official devices.

One obvious place for the writer to work in is the university, and most serious writers are now university employees, at least in the summer. Of course there is no reason why a university should employ writers who are not scholars or teachers, and not all good writers are. Still, if it does employ a good writer, it also recognizes his social importance, and it covers his freedom with its own academic freedom.

A writer who does not feel that he is developing as well as reflecting public taste will lose his self-respect very quickly. In the mass media of radio and television, as everywhere else, the democratic way is a middle way between rigid control and the anarchy of laissez-faire. This applies also to the grants for writers through wealthy foundations which help them to devote a certain amount of free time to writing. Such assistance only goes so far, but here is still another way of recognizing the importance of the writer without trying to control what he says. Sometimes it may be a very moderate talent that is being encouraged, but you never know: if such a grant had been made to Keats in the summer of 1819 the whole sensibility of the modern world might have been very different. In all these fields democracy has to follow its own trial-and-error, inductive, illogical and well-meaning way. It will not solve large problems by this method, but it will do a great deal of piece-

meal good. And as with the Canada Council Act we enter a new era
in the recognition of culture by society, we may keep in mind the
shrewd advice of William Blake:

> He who would do good to another must do it in Minute
> Particulars; General Good is the plea of the scoundrel, hypocrite
> and flatterer.

Children in Canadian schools study Canadian geography,
not because it is better than the geography of other nations, but
because it is theirs: and similarly with Canadian history and
politics. Canadian writing, too, has a value for Canadians
independent of its international value. It tells us how Canadian
imaginations have reacted to their environment, and therefore it
tells us something about Canada that nothing else can tell us. Even
if it were not very good in itself, still a Canadian who did not know
something of his own literature would be as handicapped as if he
had heard of Paris and Rome but never of Ottawa. The study of
Canadian literature is not a painful patriotic duty like voting, but
a simple necessity of getting one's bearings.

It is reasonable to assume that most Canadian literature
would be roughly Canadian in subject-matter, not because it
ought to be, but because a serious writer finds it easier to write if he
knows what he is talking about. It is often assumed that there is
something unique, or at least distinctive, about the Canadian
environment or character, and that it is the duty of our writers to
interpret those distinctive qualities. Well, this is, of course, the
most hackneyed problem in Canadian culture: all our intellectuals
are thoroughly tired of it, and very suspicious of attempts to revive
it. But they would not feel tired or suspicious if it were or ever had
been a genuine problem. The question is put the wrong way
round. Writers don't interpret national characters; they create
them. But what they create is a series of individual things, characters in novels, images in poems, landscapes in pictures. Types and
distinctive qualities are second-hand conventions. If you see what
you think is a typical Englishman, it's a hundred to one that
you've got your notion of a typical Englishman from your second-
hand reading. It is only in satire that types are properly used: a
typical Englishman can exist only in such figures as Low's
Colonel Blimp. If you look at A.Y. Jackson's paintings, you will
see a most impressive pictorial survey of Canada: pictures of

Georgian Bay and Lake Superior, pictures of the Quebec Lauren-
tians, pictures of Great Bear Lake and the Mackenzie river. What
you will not see is a typically Canadian landscape: no such place
exists. In fiction too, there is nothing typically Canadian, and
Canada would not be a very interesting place to live in if there
were. Only the outsider to a country finds characters or patterns of
behavior that are seriously typical. *Maria Chapdelaine* has something of this typifying quality, but then *Maria Chapdelaine* is a
tourist's novel.

I insist on this point because it's a special case of widespread
misunderstanding about literature. It is often believed that a new
environment is a creative influence: that because we have a lot of
new things and experiences in Canada, we ought to have a new
literature too. So we ought, except that novelty relates to content,
not to form or technique. Form and technique don't exist outside
literature, and a writer's technical power will depend, not on new
experience or new feelings, but only on how well he can absorb
what he reads. A hundred years ago Canada was a much newer
experience than it is now, and critics were predicting that new
Iliads and heroic sagas would emerge from the virgin forests. But
what the poets produced was faint echoes of Tom Moore and a few
bits of Byron and Wordsworth, because that was what they had
absorbed from their reading. That is why the ultimate standards of
Canadian literature have to be international ones. The forms in
which Canadian writers must write are established in the literary
world as a whole, chiefly in Great Britain and the United States for
writers in English. The independent value of Canadian culture for
Canadians that I just spoke of doesn't excuse the Canadian writer
from being judged by world standards. So a good deal of serious
Canadian writing is likely to seem like second-hand echoes of
American and British writers, who are not only remote from the
Canadian scene but often seem to be unreasonably difficult in
themselves. Many people in that case would be apt to feel that if the
Canada Council encourages the sort of culture that only a small
minority can understand, or if it only helps Canadians to imitate
writers who have nothing to do with Canada, it can only widen the
gap between the Canadian writer and his public. I am not
speaking of the yahoos who sound off about feeding arty bums at
the public trough and so forth; I am speaking of what a responsible citizen might reasonably feel.

This raises the question of how far a serious Canadian literature can also be popular, in the sense of being a genuine possession
of its people. There are several kinds of popular literature. One
kind is the commercial or best-seller type of popular book, usually
fiction; its popularity depends on its news value, and when that
dies the book dies too. Or it depends on sexual stimulation, which
is equally short-lived, as most of you have already discovered.
Then there is the kind of book that appeals to the eternal bourgeois
in the heart of man, the book that tells him how to get ahead in life
and supplies him with inspiring slogans and proverbial
philosophy. Books on the power of positive thinking and on
winning friends and influencing people have been popular since
the days of ancient Egypt: an eighteenth-century example was
called "The Way to be Rich and Respectable," which is as good a
title as any. Devotees of these books attach an exaggerated
importance to such poems as Kipling's *If* or Longfellow's *Psalm
of Life*, which represents the same kind of thing in poetry. There
seems to be an inner law that prevents this proverbial philosophy
from getting beyond a certain point of literary merit. I once heard a
speaker recommending Shakespeare as a poet who said profound
things about life, but this was the kind of poetry he liked, and I
couldn't help noticing that all his quotations were from Polonius
and Iago.

But there is another kind of popular literature which is more
important. This comes into the reading and listening of the child,
in the songs and the stories, the history and the wisdom, which are
central in our cultural tradition. Whatever literature we learn
early, from pre-school nursery rhymes to high-school Shakespeare
and beyond, provides us with the keys to nearly all the imaginative
experience that it is possible for us to have in life. The central part
of this training consists of the Bible, the Classics, and the great
heritage of our mother tongue. Such education includes genuinely
popular literature: that is, literature which provides a simple and
direct form of imaginative experience. In America this would
include Rip van Winkle and Huckleberry Finn, the songs of
Foster, the tall tales of the West and the comic strips that develop
similar folklore cycles in the Tennessee hills and the Florida
swamps. We have very little of it in Canada independent of its
North American context. The popular in this sense is the contemporary primitive, what in previous ages was folk song and folk

tale. Much of it is rubbish, and it includes the cheap fiction and comic books that the enormous maw and the ostrich digestion of a ten-year-old reader assimilates after school hours.

What is popular, in the sense of being permanently and genuinely well loved, is a by-product of education, and as one's education improves, the quality of what one likes improves too, until we reach the fully mature level at which the Bible and Shakespeare and the other staples of culture are popular. A good deal of the worry over the ten-year-old's comic books would be far better expended on making sure that the central educational structure is a sound one. I recently heard of a grade-eight teacher in an expensive regressive school in New York, welcoming a boy who had been away with some joke about the prodigal's return, and gradually realizing that no one in her class had heard the story of the prodigal son. Now a grade-eight student who does not know that story has not simply missed out on a piece of information that can be supplied at any time. He has been deprived of one of the keys to the whole imagination and thought of western culture, no less than if he had been deprived of the multiplication table. An educational theory which does not recognize this is not just a mistaken theory: it is criminally negligent.

If his elementary education is sound, no student will find contemporary literature remote from him. On the contrary, he will realize that T.S. Eliot and William Faulkner and Dylan Thomas have far more in common with popular literature, as I have defined it, than any positive thinker could ever have. But by this time he is beginning to feel something of the weight and power of the forces at work in society that are trying to prevent him from getting educated. Contemporary culture is very obviously about us, and it talks to us in a fully mature way. Society consists largely of adolescents and arrested adolescents, and departments of education who have to arrange high-school curricula are well aware of the fact. As a rule a student has to get to university before he can make much contact with the culture of his own time.

This suggests that much of what is now central in our cultural tradition was in its day equally disturbing in its impact, and still can be. The earliest of the prophets of Israel, we are told, was Amos, and the Book of Amos includes a few of the agonized squeals of his contemporaries: "the land is not able to bear all his words," they said. That has been the history of great culture ever since. When Wordsworth said:

We must be free or die, who speak the tongue
That Shakespeare spake; the faith and morals hold
That Milton held.

he meant what he said and he was telling the truth. But school texts of Shakespeare continue to be expurgated, for this fair land is still unable to bear all Shakespeare's words; the faith and morals of Milton are as violently resented today as they ever were. If we subsidize our culture properly, we are certain to encourage a good deal that will be described by a good many people as everything from longhair to filthy. If you think that society has outgrown such narrow-mindedness, I would call your attention to the fact that Canada, like all other countries, has laws of book censorship that no serious student of literature can possibly have the slightest respect for.

Being dissatisfied with society is the price we pay for being free men and women. And that should help us to understand the Canadian writer better, because he's so often forced to say most loudly what his audience least wants to hear. If people are morally smug, they will think their writers blasphemous; if they are sodden with integration and adjustment, they will think their writers neurotic; if they accept a way of life, they will think their writers subversive. Sometimes, of course, they will be right, but their rightness is not important, and poems which are immoral or hopelessly obscure today may be babbled happily from infant lips tomorrow. Whatever people do, most of their best writers will be doing the opposite. And if the worst of all came upon us, if we had to fight to the last ditch for our freedom, with our brothers killed and our cities in smoking ruins, our poets would still stand over against us, and break out in hymns to the glory of God and in praise of his beautiful world.

The Teacher's Source of Authority

I want to consider the question of authority in education more particularly in connection with my own subject, which is the Humanities. In the Sciences, which deal primarily with man's relation to nature, the question of authority is more or less taken care of by such things as repeatable experiment and the possibility of prediction. If an astronomer can predict an eclipse to within a second, the question of authority is inevitably bound up with his method, and there is no use arguing about the validity of observations which lead to a prediction as impressive as that. But the Humanities belong to the world which man himself creates; consequently some kind of fundamental questioning of postulates is built into them from the beginning.

Many of our ideas on education derive from Plato and from the figure of Socrates which is so important in Plato. What Plato writes is normally in the form of dialogue, and the dialogue takes the form very frequently of what he calls the symposium, a group of people meeting together at a banquet and putting forward partial and individual views of a certain central theme (such as that of love in the dialogue called *The Symposium*), with the hope that this theme will manifest itself with all the vividness and impressiveness of a Platonic form or idea in the middle of society. In his last and most complicated work, *The Laws*, Plato begins unexpectedly with the symposium as something which has a crucial importance in the actual regulating of society. He says that the symposium is an important element in education and is to that extent one of the ways of achieving the vision of authority which underlies the *Laws*. It seems extraordinary that the symposium should be used in this way in a work as serious and as comprehensive as *The Laws*, because elsewhere, Plato is quite clear about the limitations of the symposium in actual practice. He knows very well that most gatherings and discussion groups of this kind are really a collection of solipsistic monologues, or else a continuous embarassed silence.

The etymology of the word "symposium", which means "drinking together", is perhaps of some significance, because in actual symposia, ninety-nine times out of a hundred, one has to be drunk in order to believe in what is going on. Nevertheless, the symposium vision in Plato still survives in the mystique of the seminar and the belief that somehow or other a discussion which begins in an unstructured way will eventually achieve structure. Fifty years ago, for example, we have Stephen Leacock saying that if he had an ideal university to found, he would get a room full of students and then go out to hire a few professors when he got around to it. Here again is the belief that the discussion group is the core of education, despite all the evidence proving that what it usually is is a pooling of ignorance.

Before Socrates, we have the pre-Socratic philosophers, such figures as Heraclitus and Pythagoras, who were not so much philosophers, in the modern sense of the word, as gurus or spiritual leaders. They uttered dark sayings like "You can't dip your foot twice in the same river" and "Don't eat beans" and their only authority, so we are told by legend at any rate, was "*Ipse dixit*", "The master says so and that's it". What there is in an educational setting of that kind is a cult of the non-explicit, and the basis of it is the assumption that we learn only from those who do not teach. That is, such advisers, or gurus, do not teach in the sense of systematically answering questions. When you answer a question, you consolidate the mental level on which the question is asked: the efforts of such spiritual advisers are rather to keep prodding the student into making more and more adequate questions, or, at any rate, less and less inadequate questions. We find this kind of guru education still going on in our day, with the fashion for yogi and Zen Buddhism. In such surroundings, the teacher is a negative focus. Zen Buddhism has a typical form of dialogue in which the student asks a deeply serious question and gets a brush-off answer. We notice that it is when the teacher becomes a negative focus of this kind that he acquires a personal authority. The teacher who refuses to answer a question has to have tremendous authority given him by his students if he is to get away with it.

This situation survives in society, that is, a teacher is given this kind of personal authority, only when what he is dealing with happens to be generally accepted in the society, or else extremely fashionable. Our modern conceptions of education begin rather with Socrates, who renounced the idea of the possession of unusual knowledge. He kept saying that he didn't know anything but that he was looking for something. Knowledge was replaced by search, and search took the form of following a verbal trail, the trail that we know as dialectic. Socrates came into society at the moment of transition from the spoken to the written word. The written word has a linear quality in it which the spoken word, which depends much more on repetition, does not have. We notice that in most Platonic dialogues, nothing really happens until somebody, usually Socrates, takes control of the discussion, and the other contributions are reduced to punctuation. That means, essentially, that whatever authority Socrates has, in a Socratic discussion, results from the breakdown of an ideal symposium of a type that almost never manifests itself in actual experience. The same thing is true, I think, of the ordinary classroom situation, where the teacher's personal authority is acquired by default. The ideal of discussion is something which, for the most part, students are not mature enough fully to participate in.

Nevertheless, the teacher-student relationship in itself is a mutually embarrassing relationship which both are trying to escape from. So we have, in the university, a young lecturer haltingly reading his lecture notes, and the gradual growth of a sense of human presence as the discussion becomes more fluent. Perhaps once or twice in a teacher's life something of what Plato meant by the symposium actually does appear and both teacher and students recognize the common authority of the subject itself and they are all united in the vision of its power. The ghost of the symposium, similarly, revives in the community of scholars, in maintaining conferences, learned journals and the like. But there is still a lack of immediacy which accounts for the presence of what I think of as the *habeas corpus* element, the necessity of producing the body and hence, of keeping people travelling over immense distances in order to maintain the physical community of scholars.

It is obvious, of course, that the primary source of authority in the Humanities, as everywhere else, is neither the teacher nor the student but the subject being taught. Every teacher who has a vocation for teaching is aware of the insidious temptation of becoming an opaque rather than a transparent medium, and becoming a personal authority, so that the authority of the subject is conveyed only through him. There is also an intense will on the part of students to make a teacher into that kind of opaque source of authority, hence we have the superstition of the inspired teacher, as though it were possible for a teacher to get inspired by anything except his own subject. But while the subject taught is obviously the primary source of the teacher's authority, that is only the first step, and what I should like to discuss with you is the question of where the subject itself gets its authority.

In the first place, we realize that whatever is genuinely educational is continuous. There is always a type of student, for whom one has a great deal of sympathy, who would like to see every lecture, every exposure to education that he has, take the form of some kind of exciting existential experience. This again is part of the mirage of the symposium which has haunted education from the earliest times. But it is clear that education is based on what the mediaeval educators called *habitus*, in the sense in which a man who can read Latin has the habit of Latin. The basis of education is the apprentice or initiatory education, the training in skill; and the only possible basis for that is a steady repetition of certain themes arranged in a linear sequence. There is, of course, such a thing as inorganic habit, which merely repeats a convention. One finds in primitive literature, for example, a convention repeated simply because that is the way in which it has always been done. The word superstition, in religion, means, essentially, something which persists out of inorganic habit, which continues to be done without any reason understood for doing it. In all societies there is a strong anxiety of continuity, with its sense that following precedent is the source of security. This is the primitive idea of wisdom. We can see traces of it in the wisdom literature of the Bible, where wisdom means essentially the doing of the tried and tested thing, the thing which has proved in experience to maintain one's stability from one day to the next. That sense of continuity goes along, of course, with a deeply conservative view of society, a sense of the authority of seniors, of prescribed curricula, of avoiding anything like a revolutionary break in society, which confronts one with a dialectic choice.

There are two levels of habit. There is the mere habit, or mechanical repetition, and there is the practice habit which is the technique of all education and is the kind of repetition that underlies the learning of every skill, such as driving a car or playing a piano. Motor skills, like piano playing and car driving, are not different in that sense from intellectual skills, because thinking is also a matter of habit and practice. How well anyone will think at any given moment will depend, like his ability to play the piano, on how much of it he has already done. The development of both motor skills and intellectual skills, through repetition, go both down and up. It goes down into the subconscious, the instinctive, the involuntary, where things that were originally a matter of conscious effort and choice become habitual and instinctive. It goes up to plateaus of understanding or increasing insight into what one is doing. The Bible tells us that this combination of effort and relaxation is even built into the work of God himself, in a ratio of six to one. There seems to be in education, therefore, an active rhythm of production and a more passive rhythm of consumption.

This has alway been recognized in the history of education, but unfortunately it has been associated with the class structure of society and made into a political allegory, so that we have traditionally in society a working class, which provides the production in society, and a leisure class, for whom the productions of society are intended and who manifest, by their leisure, the fruits and the blessings of civilization, including education. Aristotle, for example, points out that the words "school" and "scholarship" are derived in Greek from the word "schole" which means "leisure" and the kind of liberal education that Plato and Aristotle are concerned with is only possible in a social class which has been freed from servile work. Similarly with the Bible, where the Apocrypha tells us that "the wisdom of the scribe cometh by opportunity of leisure, and he that hath little business shall become wise". The verse in the Psalms, "Be still (and know that I am God)", is, in the Septuagint, *Scholasate*, which means "have leisure" or "take your time", as though that were the foundation of a religious consciousness as well.

This tradition still survives in the nineteenth century, where the conception of the gentleman in Newman and Arnold obviously has a class reference, and it survives in our own day in the physical withdrawal from society which young people make at university. For Matthew Arnold, the conception of culture was associated with leisure and therefore with the leisure class, although Arnold saw it as operating dialectically, tending to neutralize class conflict and eventually leading us towards a classless society. But this kind of middle-class vision of education as centred in a leisurely or gentlemanly class was meeting with a good deal of resistance even then. We have, for example, William Morris, a socialist, a Marxist sympathizer, setting out in *News from Nowhere* an ideal of education which was really founded, like so much of the later philosophy of the Dewey school, on motor activity as an educational model. In Morris' ideal world of the future, everybody is engaged in cultivating the minor arts of carving and drawing. They also do a certain amount of heavier work but the sense of reflection, of contemplation, of the whole speculative side of education, is quite deliberately minimized in Morris' vision.

Here we have an example of something that runs all through the history of thought, the fact that in this area of thinking the important thing is to get hold of the right metaphors, diagrams and analogies. This educational analogy is clearly that of the human body, where the hands are the active principle and the brain, with its eyes and ears, represents something in the seat of judgment with a superior authority to the effort of working society. But not everybody has felt that this association of the leisurely aspect of education with the brain was the right metaphor. In Shakespeare's *Coriolanus*, for example, the main theme is the class struggle of the patricians and plebeians in ancient Rome. A spokesman for the patricians tries to rationalize the rule of patricians by the fable of the belly and the members, which comes from Aesop. The members of the body, we're told, rebelled against the belly but eventually they realized that they couldn't get along without the belly; a productive society cannot do without a consumer class.

The importance of this metaphor, for me, is in the suggestion that the real place for this kind of leisure is not on top, in the set of judgment, but below. What the fable attempts to prove is that the belly is not really parasitic but digestive: if so, its place is below the work of society, consolidating its efforts from time to time. What we are coming to, I think, is the fact that in our own society, these conceptions of different classes, a working class and a leisure class, are becoming simply metaphors for what are actually two aspects of every concerned and adult citizen. We have already got to the point where the phrase "leisure class" makes no sense. Perhaps our grandchildren will be living in a world in which the phrase "working class" makes even less sense.

Liberal education, then, is not a middle class privilege, but the art of setting both the individual and society free. The movement towards freedom, in this sense, is the opposite of what Matthew Arnold meant by doing as one likes, because doing as one likes means getting pushed around by one's inner compulsions. In Milton's *Areopagitica* the remark is made in passing that reason is but choosing, and this remark so impressed Milton's God that he does Milton the honour of quoting him in the speech which he makes in the third book of *Paradise Lost*. But to say only that reason is but choice seems a trifle oversimplified even for God. One wonders what the choice is, and it is clear that in the context of Milton's whole thought, choice means the choice for freedom. This is not the same thing as free choice, because free choice indicates that freedom is built into the situation from the beginning, and for Milton it is not. Adam in the Garden of Eden is confronted with the necessity of either preserving his freedom or throwing it away and his real act would have been to preserve it. What he had to preserve was the Garden of Eden itself which surrounded him on all sides.

The implication is that what really occupies the place of the brain, the seat of judgment, the ultimate source of authority, is a kind of informing vision above action. For example, a social worker trying to work in Toronto obviously has all his or her activity motivated by an inner vision of a healthier, cleaner, less neurotic and less prejudiced Toronto than the one which he or she is actually working in. Without that vision, the whole point of the work being done would be lost; hence it is in the informing vision of action that the real source of authority in education is to be found. It is to be found in the suspension of judgment that precedes the actual judgment, the choice. It is in that assembling of the materials for choice which made John Stuart Mill base his whole theory of liberty on the conception of freedom of thought, and it is that informing vision which marks the moments of genuine inspiration in the arts, those moments when the creative artist feels that somehow he is in full possession of his vision and that nothing can go wrong. Here we have the two elements of the decision maker and the adviser.

Again, in the history of education, these have been represented by social metaphors. In the Renaissance, for example, the theory of education was largely based on the education of the king, because he was the most important person to get educated. Beyond the king was the courtier, the subject of Castiglione's book, which is not only one of the most beautiful books in the world, but perhaps one of the two or three genuinely great treatises on education. The courtier's function is, of course, to become an adviser. Once again, the king and the courtier in our society are metaphors for two elements within each concerned citizen, and they refer to the different kinds of authority which are traditionally described as "de facto" authority and "de jure" authority. The "de facto" authority is where the necessity for making decisions comes in, but beyond that there is the "de jure" authority which is pre-eminently the authority in education.

The characteristic of "de facto" authority is that it always involves some kind of subordination. We often think of freedom as what the individual wants to do minus what society will stop him from doing, and even when there is no king or ruling class, there is still the sense of subordinating oneself to a "de facto" authority. "De jure" authority is a kind of authority which, like the authority of the repeatable experiment or the great work of the creative imagination, does not diminish but enhances the dignity of everyone who assents to it.

In the study of literature, for example, we begin with a response to an individual poem, then we normally go on to the total body of that poet's work, and then on to the total body of literary experience of which the poet's work forms part. Here again there is something corresponding to the ghost of the symposium which so seldom appears. The ideal literary response is a definitive experience, a response which incorporates the whole energy and power of the work of art itself. But in ordinary experience, we almost never attain such a response. We are always reading *Paradise Lost* with a hangover or seeing a performance of *King Lear* with an incompetent Cordelia; there is always something wrong with the moment of response. Hence criticism grows up as a kind of analogy of that wonderful definitive response that our actual responses all circle around, but seldom if ever, or perhaps once in a life-time, can attain.

It is only when we get to the point of having some sense of the total subject in our minds that we begin to recognize the source of an authority beyond that, of the poet or the creative artist whose work we are studying. If we are listening to music, let us say, on the level of Bach or Mozart, the response keeps shifting from the personal to the impersonal. On the one hand we feel that this is Bach, that it couldn't possibly be anybody else. On the other hand, there are moments when Bach disappears, and what we feel is: this is the voice of music itself; this is what music was created to say. At that level, we are not hearing the music so much as recognizing it. The same thing happens in the literary arts. If, in watching a play of Shakespeare on the stage, we ask what the source of authority of this dramatic structure is, we answer loudly and confidently, "Shakespeare" and we get a visual impression of the poet Shakespeare writing in his garret in Elizabethan London. The two contemporary representations of him both make him look like an idiot, so we tend to substitute the later faked portraits with their noble brow and their serene expression as the symbol of the authority that we're in touch with. But at a certain point that vanishes too and we begin to realize that this is what words have been created or invented to say. At that point, we begin to establish a kind of contact with the work of art in which authority becomes intelligible. It was a major breakthrough in literary criticism when Freud recognized in Sophocles' play of *Oedipus Rex* that working out of a situation which everybody goes through at some time or other in their lives. In other words, what the drama presents to us is the mirror of experiences which we have in some sense or other lived through ourselves. Bernard Shaw remarks of Claudius in *Hamlet* that the reason why Claudius is so fascinated by the mousetrap play is not because it's a great play, but because it's about him.

Some time ago, I was in Osaka in Japan watching a performance of the Bunraku or puppet theatre. Each puppet is manoeuvred by three attendants and the speaking parts are all taken by a speaker off-stage. After four or five hours of this, something suddenly occurred to me which I will give you in precisely the same absurd way in which it occurred to me. It seemed to me that these puppets were quite certain that they themselves were producing all the movements and noises that the audience was hearing, even though the audience could see that they were not. And that suddenly connected in my mind with my experience, for example, of the great romances of Shakespeare's period: *The Winter's Tale, The Tempest, Cymbeline,* where the characters seem to me to have been deliberately scaled down to puppet size. Again, they seem quite certain that they are autonomous sources of what they are doing, even though it is obvious that some divinity off-stage, like Jupiter in *Cymbeline,* or someone else on-stage, like Prospero in *The Tempest,* was producing it all for them.

And that in turn begins to dramatize, so to speak, the situation of drama itself. Here again, we have, as we have in the theory of education, the actors and the watchers, the players and the audience. The watcher knows more, and that fact is the source of all irony in drama. The audience always knows more about what is happening than the players on the stage do, and because the audience can walk out of the theatre at the end, they're also in a situation of greater freedom. What they are looking at in the play on the stage is a recognition of patterns that they themselves contain. Our own experience tells us that we spend our lives acting out roles and assuming one persona after another. There are pathetic illusions about encounter groups, which are supposed to get underneath a persona to the real person, but there is never anything under a persona except another persona; there is no core to that onion. The process of playing roles is infinite, and, as Hamlet's soliloquies demonstrate, we keep on dramatizing ourselves to ourselves.

So drama, which I'm taking as central form of literary education, is not only a training in the ancient axiom of knowing oneself, but also a training in something which the existentialists tell us is impossible: of being a spectator of one's own life, of developing that kind of creative schizophrenia in which one can both act and watch oneself acting at the same time. So it seems that there are, in addition to the steady effort, the forming of habit, in the learning process, elements which (again using diagrams and metaphors) are both below it and above it. The one below it is what the cultivated man gets, a possession of rarefied pleasure usually dependent on a certain kind of class structure. It is something which he can use and which can give pleasure and even serenity to his life, but it has no power to transform him. On the upper level is that descending informing vision which is what Heidegger is pointing to when he says that man does not use language but responds to language. Man obviously does use language, but he does so only on the level of personal cultivation, the leisure which Menenius in *Coriolanus* tells us is centred in the belly and not the brain.

We are all born under a social contract; we belong to something before we are anything, and that is the source of all the "de facto" authority which exists in a context of subordination. But the society of this social contract is only the transient appearance of society, a society in which a single psychotic with a rifle can change the Presidency of the United States, and in which empires rise and fall as rapidly as women's hem lines. It is clear that such a society has only an interim and emergency authority. Behind the transient appearance of society are the permanent realities of the arts and sciences which education leads us to. It is obvious, therefore, that the social contract has to be supplemented by an educational contract. This latter is the recognition of the reality behind the transient appearances presented in our morning newspapers and television, and it is the contract with an authority which does not diminish, but emancipates.

Every great writer, we notice, has two forms of communication; he meant something to his own time, and he means something to us across great barriers of time and space and language. He communicates to us for reasons often quite different from those which appealed to his own day. Our twentieth century understanding of Shakespeare is quite different from the Elizabethan understanding of Shakespeare, and if there is one thing certain about the body of Shakespearean criticism in the twentieth century, it is that Shakespeare himself would have found it unintelligible. But the fact that these double appeals, to one's own time and to our time, have to keep polarizing each other in a continued tension, leads us to a glimpse into what the permanence of the society represented by the arts and sciences really is. It is a glimpse beyond the tyranny of an irreversible time and the temporary expediencies which are the normal form of life in the ordinary world, into a world which has an authority because it lies beyond our ordinary mental capacities of time and space, and hence leads us to understand how we can be what Proust calls "giants immersed in time".

III

The Social Order

The Definition of a University

In a recent interview connected with this essay I was asked why I wanted to present a definition of the university to an audience that might not be profoundly interested in the subject. I suggested that there were two reasons. First, the superstitions and the pseudo-concepts of educational methodology have not made much impact on the university, at least so far, and consequently the university can still serve as a model of educational aims. The second and more important reason, I said, is that, being a voluntary enterprise, at least technically, the university does not have the penal quality which universal compulsory education necessarily has attached to it. The word "penal" slipped out without my intending it, and I wondered afterwards why I had used a word which might possibly be offensive.

As I began to think about this, certain visions of my own childhood days arose in my mind. I saw children lined up and marched into a grimy brick building at nine in the morning, while a truant officer prowled the streets outside. The boys and the girls were sent in through sexually separated entrances: it was regarded as a matter of the highest importance that a boy should not go through a door marked "girls" even if no act of excretion was involved. They then filed into their classrooms, found their desks and sat down with their hands folded in front of them in what was referred to as "sitting position". At that point a rabble of screaming and strapping spinsters was turned loose on them, and the educational process began. The deterrent to idleness, in this setup, was being kept in, or having one's sentence lengthened. As the students grew older, the atmosphere of the classroom came to resemble that of an armed truce. There was a high correlation between a boy's ability to disturb a classroom and his popularity with his classmates, as he himself well knew. The boys, for the most part, resisted the educational process openly, their resistance being either sullen or boisterous, depending on temperament. The girls, on the other hand, were far more docile; they tended to be obedient and to do as they were told. It was many years before I realized that docility was by far the more effective form of resistance.

I remember a good deal of unconscious sadism on both sides— teachers as well as students. But there was not, of course, the built-in brutality that goes with teaching younger members of a ruling class, and that belongs to expensive and exclusive public schools. I remember that I had a good deal of sympathy and some liking for my teachers, but I think only one of them was an influence on me. That was my music teacher, with whom I had a purely voluntary and extracurricular connection. He had no truant officer behind him, but he did have the only authority that matters—the authority that springs from a genuine knowledge and love of his subject. The last time I went to see him, he was still dwelling on what had been obviously one of the happiest evenings of his life, an evening during the war when two desperately lonely British airmen, stationed at a camp nearby, had phoned and said, "We hear you're a musician. Is it all right if we come up just to talk about music?"

Now you will say that this picture is a very different one from what you remember, to say nothing of what those of you who are teachers would want to produce in your own classrooms. There has been a good deal of change. There should have been in forty years. I will come to the reasons for some of the change later. But there has been a good deal of continuity too.

I find that I think very little about my school days, but that I think much more about the kind of society which lay behind the school and the kind of assumptions it had built into it, conscious and unconscious. For example: one of the things that bored me to death with public schools was the fact that our text books were so grotesquely out of date. In the twenties of this century, our geography book talked of Germany's "newly acquired province of Alsace-Lorraine", and the maps were of the same vintage. The British history was written by someone who was not quite certain of the outcome of the Boer War. The physiology book explained with diagrams how women distorted their viscera by tight lacing, and the physics book talked glibly about ether. This was, I recognize, a purely local flowering of incompetence, and it would not have had its direct counterpart elsewhere. Nevertheless, it comes close to the two permanent defects in education. One is the pathetic illusion that new methods of teaching can make up for an out-of-date conception of the subject, or for a steadily increasing ignorance of the subject. Publishers understand this illusion very well, and they continually push new gimmicks because they realize that a genuinely new conception of a subject would cause immediate panic. This is why every week I get brochures for text books on literary criticism based on conceptions of literary theory that would have been antiquated to Samuel Johnson and primeval to Coleridge.

The other assumption which allowed such textbooks to exist was, I think, even more important. This was a feeling that children ought to be kept off the streets not only physically but mentally. This assumption is related to that curious conception of the limbo of "adolescence"—the conception that there ought to be a period of life, between puberty and voting age, in which young people should be, to some extent, segregated from what is going on in the world. This conception of the adolescent can hardly have any basis in biology: it is a deliberate creation of industrial society, and one wonders why such a creation was made. One frequent explanation, the one advanced by Robert Hutchins, is that the reason is economic. The attempt is to slow down productivity, or as Hutchins says, to turn American education into a gigantic play-pen in order to keep young people off the labour market. I think this is quite possibly a part of the explanation, but by no means the whole of it. I want to return to this question: meanwhile, I should like to make it clear that when I use the word "adolescent", I do not refer primarily to young people, but to a social neurosis which has been projected on young people.

Some of the things that I learned at school were not what I was intended to learn. There was a barrage of propaganda directed against smoking and drinking, which, so far as I could gather, had no effect whatever on the mores of the community, a large proportion of which drank its way all through Prohibition with the greatest enthusiasm. I dare say that similar propaganda against drugs goes on in the schools now, even in communities where half the population is employed in pushing drugs at the other half. What I learned was that propaganda is entirely useless unless it can suggest some kind of participatory role for those at whom it is addressed. It is not because the propaganda was negative that it was ineffective. Negative propaganda can, unfortunately, sometimes be very effective. In Nazi Germany it was possible to convince German children that Jews were of a different human type from themselves, even though their senses and their reason were telling them the opposite. But propaganda based merely on the "don't do that" formula is clearly wasted effort.

The schools were also designed to teach what was referred to as good grammar, that is, a standard English which no one spoke or even tried to speak. I remember one remark of a teacher, "Tomorrow we will go on to the lesson on 'shall' and 'will', because I would like to finish it by Friday". The language of the recess ground was unaffected by the learned language, partly for class reasons: colloquial language was the reassuring speech of those who belonged; "good grammar" represented the unpopular minority cult of intellect and culture. I noted too that two things which were rigidly excluded from all our reading material were the themes of sex and violence. I began to understand why sex and violence are the most genuinely popular elements of popular culture.

Why was there so little sense of participation? I think it was partly because of another unconscious assumption on the part of society, that Johnny should go to school because it was natural for him not to want to. That is, what he naturally wanted to do, according to this assumption, was play, and to be sent to school was enrolling him in a civilized operation. Civilization, then, was assumed to be antagonistic to nature. This assumption, that civilization takes the form of an authoritarian domination of nature, is exactly the same assumption which has produced, in other aspects of our society, the tedious grid pattern of our streets, our countrysides, and now even of our buildings. The same assumption is behind our pollution problems, behind the almost unimaginable hideousness of urban sprawl, behind the wanton destruction of trees and rivers and animals. There, if I had had eyes to see it, was the central paradox of the contemporary world. It was all around me at school, and it was still all around me after I went to college, enrolled in a course in philosophy, and settled down to grapple with some of its primary texts, including Aristotle's *Metaphysics*, the first sentence of which reads, "All men by nature desire to know".

It is customary when a class is ready to leave school or college to ask a convocation speaker to come and tell them that they have now finished their education and are ready to go out into the world. I have a genuine sympathy with convocation speakers, because I have probably made as many speeches in my time as anyone else in the country, but that is one theme that I have never used. It is obvious that nobody ever goes into the world at all, and that when one is ready to leave school the social order simply picks him up and drops him into a different file. We leave school and we get a job, and the job is psychologically identical with the school as I have described it. The job is nearly always penal: it is endured so that one can enjoy one's spare time outside it without crippling anxiety, and perhaps with some hope of getting more spare time as one becomes more senior. But from Biblical times there has been a tendency to regard work as partial reparation for what the soul in a poem of Yeats calls "the crime of birth".

The motive behind compulsory universal education was on the whole a benevolent one. The motive was that in a democracy one had to be trained to participate in a very complex society. At the age of six one may think that one does not want the training, but one will want it later. Education which seems to the child irrelevant is not really irrelevant so much as tentative. A girl in high school may feel that she can't do algebra because it does not correspond to the vision of the kind of life she thinks she wants to lead. But the community mildly compels her to try a little algebra, because this is a democracy, and it is her right to be exposed to quadratic equations however little she wants them. And still what all this benevolence has produced in society is a kind of maximum security prison, maximum because it is impossible to escape to the world outside. There is no world outside. There was once a convict at Alcatraz who got out of the prison library a book of poems, opened it and saw the two lines of a poem by Lovelace: "Stone walls do not a prison make, nor iron bars a cage". He looked around him and said, "Well, if that's true, this is one damn good imitation." Yet I think the poet was right as well as the inmate. A prison is any enclosure that gives claustrophobia to those who are inside it. We meet this sense of claustrophobia everywhere in society. So the question arises, "How did benevolence produce a prison?"

I begin my approach to this by distinguishing and contrasting two different kinds of habit or repetition. There is one kind of habit or repetition which is the basis of the whole learning process. It is the habit of practice, of progress through repeated, sometimes mechanically repeated, effort, which we see in anyone who is learning to play the piano or memorize the multiplication table. It is habit in the medieval sense of *habitus*, in which a man who could read Latin was said to have the habit of Latin, that is, he had practised Latin and had repeated the practice until he had it in his mind. There was a man in New York who lost his way in Manhattan, stopped an old lady and said, "How do I get to Carnegie Hall?" The old lady said, "Practise, practise." Practise in this sense is the basis of all mental activity and of all creative activity as well.

But there is another kind of habit or repetition which is exactly the opposite. This is the kind of anxiety-habit which is created by the fact that we change roles so frequently during the course of a day, often to the point of feeling that our identity is threatened. So we adopt ritual patterns of behaviour, patterns of compulsive repetition, in order to establish a sense of continuous identity in our minds. This pattern of repetition which is inorganic, which is clung to out of fear, is one which gradually moves us further and further from what we are in contact with. Thus the benevolence which produced the compulsory universal education bill became habitual, and, because it was habitual, it became binding. Conditions change, and when attitudes towards those conditions do not change, there comes a curious Hegelian fatality into human life of eventually producing the opposite of what was originally aimed at. One example would be the career of President Nixon, who was elected on a promise that he would try to unite the country, and who within two years came to a position in which he could keep going only by trying to divide it. A different kind of example is afforded by the relations of Canada and the United States. When the United States invaded Canada in 1812, it ran into a strong separatist sentiment and some well-organized guerrilla tactics. The Americans failed to conquer Canada as ignominiously as they have failed to conquer North Vietnam. So they opted for peace and an undefended border, with the result that Canada is today almost the only country in the world which is a pure colony, a colony psychologically as well as economically. It has now the same relation to the United States that the United States had to Great Britain before 1776, except for the revolutionary sentiment.

This phenomenon of things reversing themselves is particularly noticeable when society fastens on to something as a symbol for its anxiety and tries to maintain it without change. A good example would be the attitude to women in middle-class Victorian society. Women in that society were made the focus of the social anxieties of their time: they were supposed to be the keepers of good manners, of proper speech and proper behaviour. Hence the conditions set up for them subordinated them under the guise of protecting them. They could not vote and, if they were married, could not own property, because they were regarded as "pure" — purity, like impurity, being a conception which always involves social segregation. The result of making women the custodians of Victorian anxieties was, of course, that that society became very largely matriarchal. Women accepted the ethos which had been handed them, and proceeded to impose it on the rest of society. I could give many examples from Victorian novels. One of the most incisive, perhaps, is in George Eliot's *Middlemarch*, which tells us how Dr. Lydgate, a brilliant scientist and a most original doctor, wanted a typically Victorian wife who would not disturb him intellectually and who would look decorative at his parties. So he married a beautiful, stupid and insipid woman who promptly took his life over, and in no time at all he had lost all his originality and his eminence as a scientist and became simply a stuffed shirt giving the kind of parties at which she could appear.

Around the time that I was going to school, society was beginning to create another focus of anxiety on the young. This was a feeling that young people ought to be left in an age of innocence before they got into the "rat race". Why should they get old before their time? Why should they take on responsibilities that they need not take on? Young people so fresh and attractive ought to be relieved from social responsibilities, and so symbolize the dream of leisure, of getting away from it all, that older people feel they have missed in life. And so there came a social system which both subordinated and protected young people, in the age group from puberty to majority, and did with adolescence substantially what the Victorian middle class had done to women. The result was the same, the growth and eventual domination of society by an adolescent ethos. This ethos now dominates the mass market, forcing women of sixty into mini-skirts; it dominates entertainment, and now it tends increasingly to dominate politics, what with kidnapping, stonethrowing, rioting and similar adolescent forms of facing reality. Again, I repeat that my term "adolescence" refers to a social fixation which is represented by young people, but does not originate with them. The youthful activist who talks about his resentment against "authoritarianism" and "establishments" and "power structures" is falling into the anxiety role prescribed for him by his elders. Hence the paradox, which of course is not really a paradox at all, that the more he asserts his equality with those of a generation older, the less of such equality he actually feels, and the more typically "adolescent" his behavior becomes.

The "adolescent" is by definition immature, and the question of maturity, therefore, becomes a major social problem. About twenty years ago there was quite a cult of maturity, and people wrote books with titles like *The Mature Mind*. (I remember one such book written by a very famous psychologist, whose name you would recognize if I gave it, in which he said that the mature way to stop war was to learn to minimize the combative impulses. That is a strong contender for the least informative sentence that I have ever read.) But the word "mature" is out of fashion now. When, for example, a university administrator is faced by a student deputation demanding the instant and total reform of something, he is strongly tempted to use the word "immature" to describe their demands. He does not do so, partly because it would only make things worse, and partly because he realizes that they don't want the reform anyway, but have merely been told to demand it by an organizer with his mind on higher things. Nevertheless, if he did use the term, it seems to me that the students would have a right to say, immature in relation to what? If by maturity you mean either being resigned to or accepting conditions in our society that we regard as foolish and evil, we don't want your maturity; we would rather be immature. Whatever one thinks of that answer, one often has to ask one's self the complementary question in a time of crisis: "Where are the mature people?"

I have lived through the People's Park crisis in Berkeley, California, which struck me as a preposterous, silly and totally unnecessary event. It would have been easy to dismiss it as an immature and irresponsible action. But who was being mature? It wasn't the university teaching staff, which was demoralized. It wasn't the police, who were being given the most incredibly stupid orders. And it certainly was not the government of the state, which showed a considerable degree of low cunning in exploiting the situation, but certainly no wisdom or courage. Similarly, the tactics of the terrorists in the F.L.Q. are, to put it mildly, immature. But whether the mixture of negligence and over-reaction that countered them was mature or not is a much more dubious question.

We have to conclude, it seems to me, that there are no mature people. Maturity is not a thing you find in people; it's a thing that you find only in certain mental processes. These mental processes are what the university is all about: the mental processes of reasoning, as distinct from rationalization, of experiment, of considering evidence, of the precise and disciplined imagination that appears in literature and the arts. These processes are the end and aim of the right kind of habit, the practice-habit on which all civilized life is founded.

We think a good deal about freedom in terms of an antithesis between what the individual wants and what society will allow him to have. We tend to think of society, therefore, as inherently repressive, and we consequently have the greatest difficulty in trying to work out the conception of a free society. This antithesis of freedom and compulsion is something that, as soon as we get into the mental processes I just mentioned, completely disappears. If an artist is painting a picture, what he wants to do and what he must do are the same thing. If a thinker says, "After considering this evidence, I am forced to the following conclusion," he does not mean that he is being externally compelled. The authority that compels him does not counteract his freedom: it fulfils his freedom and it is the same thing as his freedom.

In later life one speaks of the great changes that one has lived through, usually congratulating one's self on one's power of surviving them. Certainly the changes that anyone of my age has gone through are very considerable. Not too long ago, the King of England was Emperor of India; Nazi Germany ruled Europe from the Atlantic to the Volga; China was a bourgeois friend, Japan a totalitarian enemy, and so on. The moral that one ought to draw from this is that what appears to be real society is not real society at all, but only the transient appearance of society. The permanent form of human society is the form which can only be studied in the arts and the sciences. Those are the genuinely organized structures of human civilization. It is in the arts and the sciences that we understand where the causes are that make society change so rapidly and seem so unpredictable. If that is true, then our definition of education has to be very different from the one that we often give. Of all the superstitions that have bedevilled the human mind, one of the most dismal and fatuous is the notion that education is a preparation for life. It was very largely this notion of education that caused the projecting of anxiety and the fear of change on the "adolescent", and on trying to maintain him in an imaginary state of innocence.

There are two forms of society, we said, the temporary and transient appearance of society which comes to us through newspapers and television, and the real structure of society which is revealed by the arts and sciences. Education, therefore, should be defined as the encounter with real life, whereas the world which involves us as citizens and taxpayers and readers of papers and people with jobs is not real life but a dissolving phantasmagoria. Of course, it is possible that this encounter with real life can go to the point of making one maladjusted to the dissolving world. This is, in fact, one of the functions of education. The last thing that education ought to try to do is to adjust anybody to the appearance of a society which will not be there by the time he has become adjusted to it. But it can and should make one to some extent maladjusted. In T.S. Eliot's phrase, "Human kind cannot bear very much reality", but without the little it can bear it cannot bear the rest of life.

Because of the traditional view, and for many historical reasons, university students have all been drawn from one age group, and hence they naturally assume that the university belongs to them. Actually the university belongs to the whole community, and I wish very much that this could be reflected in the make-up of the student body in the university. I am not speaking of adult education: I am speaking of a full re-entry into the university by people in their thirties and forties and fifties, teachers who need refresher courses in their profession, business men who need refresher courses outside their profession, married women with grown-up families, and many other people who have had some earlier encounter with the university, but have forgotten the content of what they have learned and recognize that they need a recurrent contact with it as their life goes on. The only real reason for wanting this is the inherent worth of the subjects themselves, but there are economic advantages as well. It would be a little easier to sell education to the taxpayer if he had some sense of personal contact with it and did not feel that he was supporting only a leisure class of young people.

This conception, of the university student body as a leisure class, is a survival of an older form of social elitism. A generation ago there were fewer students in universities: it did not follow, however, that those who were there were all highly intelligent. It followed, rather, that those who were there were people of good intelligence who belonged to the middle class. A century ago the goal of university education was defined by Newman as, in the broadest sense, a social goal, as having the function of producing in society what Newman called the "gentleman". But it is clear that "gentleman" is no longer a socially functional conception, and the notion of the "best" education as being only of the kind that the university confers is obviously a considerable social nuisance in our day.

I have taught relatively few older people in universities. I remember however a class in Shakespeare in which there was one man of about fifty. We were discussing *Measure For Measure* and the complicated character of its heroine Isabella. He came up to me afterwards and said, "You know, I couldn't say this in front of the class, but they all think Isabella is a grown woman, but she's not, She's a teenager. Look at the way she's crazy to go into a convent. You know, they all go through that stage." I thought that this was a fresh and candid comment on *Measure For Measure*, and I could understand why he communicated it to me in this confidential way. But it seems to me that if his age group had been more fairly represented in the class, there might perhaps have been a more understanding discussion between the two groups about what "teenagers" thought and why.

One reason why I feel the university should be deeply concerned with the education of older people is that so much technical training has such a short life, including the training of teachers and whatever undergraduate training one may have had thirty years back. It is not always understood that the research training in university graduate schools can go out of date just as quickly. As a colleague of mine remarked to me of another colleague's book, "You know, that book would have been pretty radical if he had written it 100 years ago." The university has to be a mixture of teaching and research functions, and the two functions have constantly to update each other. A teacher who is not a scholar is soon going to be out of touch with his own subject, and a scholar who is not a teacher is soon going to be out of touch with the world.

I have spoken of a kind of social elitism still persisting in our society after it has become functionally obsolete. We speak, for example, of "only a few" being capable of doing university work, and forget that, in a world as populous as ours, "only a few" can still mean a great many million. Then again, there is the mystique, as I might call it, of the small staff/student ratio. On the part of students, the belief that education is always better when there are very few students to one instructor, and when there is greatest freedom and variety of choice, is a false analogy with participatory democracy. On the part of the staff, it is a survival of the notion that teaching is an evil necessary to support research, that one's ambition ought to be to teach one's own speciality, and that the fewer students you have, the higher your status ought to be. Both of these are leisure-class attitudes. It seems to me that all subjects of research do not necessarily have to be taught, and I should think that there would be many pedagogical advantages in a drastic simplification of the curriculum. Here again, though the pedagogical reasons are the only important ones, there would be economic fringe benefits, as simplifying the curriculum is the only real way to save money in higher education.

As for small classes, the tutorial system is of course greatly admired, especially by those who have never been exposed to it. But the tutorial system with all its virtues cannot give a panorama or perspective as a lecture can do. There is a corresponding mystique of the seminar. The seminar certainly has a central place in education, and should be there, and very prominently there, from the age of twelve to the time of the PhD. At the same time, students expect and ought to get something better from their tuition fees than merely the sound of their own ignorance coming back from the four walls. The development of fluency is also an ambiguous benefit. I have known graduates of several colleges in the United States that made a special technique of dealing with very few students at a time and teaching them to talk by means of seminars, and the echo of their horrid articulateness still rings in my ears. It seems to me that nobody should be trained to talk unless he is simultaneously trained to listen, because, if he is, then what is called "dialogue" simply becomes a series of solipsistic monologues, and any gathering of people will take on that form of group psychosis which can be studied in almost any conference called in the modern world. As for the analogy from democracy, the essential democratic principle in education is the supremacy of the subject over both the teacher and the student, and the more supreme it is, the more the difference between the teacher and the student is minimized. The implementation of democracy in the classroom comes from the teacher's willingness to share his knowledge and the student's willingness to acquire it, and the authority of the subject corresponds to the authority in democratic society of (if you will pardon what is by now a somewhat coarse expression) law and order.

If the teaching and learning conditions of the university approached at all to the conditions which I have outlined, I should like to see them extended further and further down into the school programme. I am aware that young children go through different stages, and we need the research of Piaget and others to tell us what those stages are and to allow for them in our teaching programme. But I have invariably found that, of the teachers that I have talked to, those who most obviously knew what they were doing were also those with the least sense of difference between what they were doing and what I was doing. The same thing is true of students. Anybody who wants a substitute mother in grade two will still be wanting one in second year university.

Throughout my professional career, I have noted that teachers are occupationally disposed to believe in magic, that is, to believe in the virtues of a planned and sequential curriculum. I share that:

I believe in such magic as firmly as any other teacher, and I have done a good deal of work on trying to plan sequential programmes in English from kindergarten to graduate school. Teachers, at least in previous years, used to do a great deal of conferring, asking one another whether a course would not be magically improved if instead of the sequence a, b, c, d one had the sequence a, d, b, c, or possibly a, c, d, b. The role of the student in all this was assumed to be roughly what Newman described in his famous hymn, "Lead Kindly Light": "I loved to choose and see my path, but now lead thou me on." Newman, however, was talking to God, who is presumably a more reliable conductor than most teachers. Students have to choose and see their path, even though most of what they see is simply the consequences of choice. The teacher, in his turn, needs to realize that a teacher cannot be taught to teach except by good students. By that I do not mean such things as student evaluation, which is a parody of genuine process, and is something for which I have no respect whatever. I am not speaking of that, but of a constant participating in the learning operation.

The increase of student representation on curricular and administrative bodies in the university is a part of the social life of our time, and no reasonable person is likely to oppose it. And yet, because it falls into the rhythm of society's movement, it tends to fall under the law of reversal which I have already mentioned. That is, as students and junior faculty become increasingly represented in a department, the department becomes so huge and cumbersome that eventually an executive committee is assigned the whole responsibility, and so the university, instead of becoming less bureaucratic and impersonal, steadily becomes more so. It does not follow that we ought to try reverse the trend to student and junior faculty representation, which would be futile nonsense. But in proportion as department and senate and council meetings become a sounding-board for professional noisemakers, and the running of the university is taken over by an increasingly invisible civil service, the real teachers and the real students will have to get together on a largely conspiratorial basis, forming small groups discussing problems of primary interest to themselves. This conspiratorial activity will be what will rebuild the university.

At the University of Toronto there used to be a distinction between a three-year general course and a four-year honour course, but this has been swept away in a great wave of exuberant hysteria.

The theories of these two courses were complementary. The theory of the general course assumed a certain coordinating of disciplines, so that the student could see a broad area of knowledge from different points of view. The principle of the honour course was that every area of knowledge is the centre of all knowledge. Both these theories may have required too much sophistication from both students and teachers, but I would hope that after the dust settles and the University becomes restructured, it will beome restructured along the older patterns.

I am often asked if a student today is different from his predecessors, and usually the answer expected is yes. The answer happens to be no. There has been a tremendous increase in the rain of sense impressions from the electronic media, and this has produced a considerable alertness and power of perception on the part of students. However, the power to integrate and coordinate these impressions is not greater than it was. This is a situation which has been interpreted by my colleague, Professor Marshall McLuhan, but I would regard his interpretation, if I have understood it correctly, as quite different from mine. He distinguishes between the linear and fragmented approach which he associates with the printed book and the total and simultaneous response which he associates with the electronic media. It seems to me, on the other hand, that it is the existence of a written or printed document that makes a total and simultaneous response possible. It stays there: it can referred to; it can become the focus of a community. It is the electronic media, I think, which have increased the number of linear and fragmented experiences—experiences which disappear as soon as one one has had them—and because of that, they have also increased the general sense of panic and dither in modern society. At the same time, there is no doubt that television and the movies have developed new means of perception, and that they indicate the need for new educational techniques which, as far as I know, have not yet been worked out. I did hear a lecture some time ago by an educator which began by showing the audience a television commercial. He then said, "There is one thing in that commercial which all of you missed and which all the young people to whom it was shown got at once." I thought to myself, "Now we're getting to something important. Now we shall find out how education is going to adjust itself to this situation." But, unfortunately, all he said after that was, "This indicates a fact of great educational importance. We don't quite know what it is, but we have it under close study."

I have spoken of the mental processes of the university as consisting of a group of things: experiment, evidence, reasoning, imagination. It is possible for different aspects of these to get out of proportion. In our day there is a tendency for one's social vision to get drowned in facts. We look at poverty and inflation and unemployment, and we feel that we can only deal with these things after we have got enough facts about them. And so we employ commissions to spend years and millions of dollars on reports, while poverty and inflation and unemployment placidly continue to rise every month. That is a disease of our time. At other times facts get squeezed out by speculative theories. Thus in the fifteenth century, for example, we had an elaborate classification of the nine orders of the angels, but no classification of rocks or geological strata. The proportioning of these things results from the kind of social vision that a community has, and the university in its totality, that is, the arts and sciences taken together, defines this social vision. It is the university's task to define the vision of society. To implement that vision is the business of concerned organizations, like churches, pressure groups and political parties. It is not the business of the university as such. In this neo-fascist age, there are many who dislike the kind of freedom which the university represents, and would like to kidnap the university by a pressure group of some kind, radical or established, according to their prejudices. But, if this happened, society's one light would go out.

I can best conclude by trying to amplify and emphasize this point. Of course I should be cutting the throat of my own argument if I were to say that the university should be protected by and subordinated to society, because that would be putting the university in exactly the same position that I have said women were in in Victorian times and adolescents in this century. If that happened the logical result would be spread of an ethos of Olympian indifference in which the answer to every problem would be, "Well, we'll have to wait and see until we have considered all the evidence". There is a good deal of this attitude around already, but when universities foster it they are, like the pure Victorian maiden or the bumptious contemporary adolescent, merely helping to dramatize a foolish role that society need never have invented in the first place.

The university belongs to its society, and the notion of autonomy of the university is an illusion. It is an illusion which it would be hard to maintain on the campus of the University of Toronto, situated as it is between the Parliament Buildings on one side and an educational Pentagon on the other, like Samson between the pillars of a Philistine temple. But the university has a difficult and delicate job to do: it is responsible to society for what it does, very deeply responsible, yet its function is a critical function, and it can fulfill that function only by asserting an authority that no other institution in society can command. It is not there to reflect society, but to reflect the real form of society, the reality that lies behind the mirage of social trends. It is not withdrawn or neutral on social issues: it defines our real social vision as that of a democracy devoted to ideals of freedom and equality, which disappears when society is taken over by a conspiracy against these things. It may be attacked from the "left", as it is when certain types of radicals demand that every professor should be, in theory, opposed to war and imperialism and laissez faire, and in practice a Marxist stooge. It may be attacked from the "right", as it was by a Toronto newspaper, which, seeing a bandwagon rolling by, printed an article asserting that professors ought to be teaching students rather than subjects (perhaps the silliest of all fallacies in a subject full of them), and reinforced this with a snarling editorial saying that professors had better reform themselves along these lines, but quick, or else "society" would do it for them. These attacks have in common the belief that "academic freedom" is an outmoded concept, dating from a time before "society" realized how easily it could destroy everything it had of any value. The university has to fight all such attacks, and in fighting them it becomes clear that the intellectual virtues of the university are also moral ones, that experiment and reason and imagination cannot be maintained without wisdom, without charity, without prudence, without courage; without infinite sympathy for genuine idealism and infinite patience with stupidity, ignorance and malice. Actually academic freedom is the only form of freedom, in the long run, of which humanity is capable, and it cannot be obtained unless the university itself is free.

The Ethics of Change

In my own university drastic proposals for curricular and other reforms are now being discussed, and while I am personally in sympathy with many of the proposals themselves, I am apprehensive of the conception of the university towards which they seem to be directed. As the Virgin Mary says in a seventeenth-century "Expostulation", I trust the god, but I fear the child. I can hardly suppose that Queen's University is not preoccupied with similar problems, so my present assignment is not rooted in the specific occasion of which I have the honour to be a part. The rhetorical style that I have chosen is the mandarin style, which seems to me appropriate to a ceremonial occasion, being out of fashion.

The ethics of change is a phrase which suggests an attempt to think about something that has already gone ahead of thought, like a car driver applying brakes in a skid. In society there is normally a conflict between two kinds of anxiety: a conservative, or let's-be-careful-about-losing-what-we've-got, anxiety, and a radical, or let's-clear-out-all-this-stuff-and-have-a-fresh-breeze-blow-through, anxiety. When one anxiety dominates the other, change is thought of as itself an ethical process, good if the radical anxiety is dominant, bad if the conservative one is. In our day we are passing through a period of dominant radical anxiety, because we feel that we have already created the conditions of a different kind of society from the one we are living in.

A literary critic gets his clues to such a situation by looking at the emotional values attached to metaphors. The metaphor of technological obsolescence meets us everywhere: there is a general panic about escaping from the obsolete. Again, liquid and gaseous metaphors ("keeping things stirred up", and the like) have a favourable context and solid ones like "standard" and "set-up" an unfavourable one. A few years ago "structure" was a magical word, but today it suggests mainly the death-watch beetle, and "unstructured" has replaced it. This metaphorical structure, or unstructure, has been developed in order to incorporate a sense of conflict between youth and age, where youth symbolizes a plastic and age a rigid element. A colleague of mine who watched the Paris student demonstrations tells me that he saw an old lady standing on the street with tears streaming down her face and shouting *"Vive la Jeunesse!"* I understand the old lady's cry very well, but I am assuming that no one in this audience is going to applaud or condemn the young, or the old, merely for being young or old. Such slogans as "never trust anyone over thirty", even when stolen from Bernard Shaw, do not seem to me very cogent, and my heart is not wrung by efforts of middle-class students, whose every opinion is respectfully considered, to compare themselves to Negro slaves. The conflict of generations is clearly projected from the self-conflicts of both generations. The aging have the fear of seeming to be no longer young in spirit which is one of the normal hazards of aging; the young the fear of the shadows of their own future selves, when they will inevitably be more committed to society.

The earliest philosopher of change was Heraclitus, who remarked simply, "Change is a rest": that is, it is in change that things find relief from being what they are. In the university, a period of rapid change is a period of the lowering of intellectual sights. It is a period of concentrating on methodology, on administration, on committee reports; a period where the action is felt to be in meetings rather than in classrooms. There is a corresponding emphasis on the assimilating of education to experience. Education is distinguished from "mere" training, or the "mere" acquiring of facts, until it gets almost disconnected from the learning process, as though intellectual curiosity did not normally express itself as a desire for knowledge. Demands for "relevance" and for "self-evaluation" tend to minimize continuity (which implies inner structure) in learning, and to emphasize the discontinuous experiences of teach-in, sit-in, confrontation, and conversation (usually called "unstructured discussion"). I am not saying that such emphases ought never to become important: I am saying that the exhilaration of rapid change, in a university, is not the exhilaration of mental adventure and progress, but of mental release and letdown.

The danger of a dominant radical anxiety is in finding in the mechanics of change a substitute for education. The "mere" acquiring of knowledge is also the only means of advance in education, its only liberalizing principle. It is the infallible sign of the anti-intellectual that he looks toward some other activity, which repeats but does not progress, which hardens attitudes and confirms prejudices, as the key to education. "Book-learning" for him ought always to be subordinated to some kind of exciting existential happening, which also helps to prevent brain fever. The present mystique of "confrontation" sessions and the like continue the attack on the learning process, and continue to support the refusal of the lotus-eaters to embark on the discovering voyage.

In my own student days in the thirties, the depression was the central social fact and most radical students were sympathetic to Marxism as then interpreted by Stalinism. The Marxist radical of the thirties accepted the work ethic as completely as any capitalist, but he sought solidarity with the working class, as he defined it. All his efforts were focussed on the moment of takeover, the point at which the political and economic structure would pass from bourgeois into working-class hands. The position of the "new left" today is very different. The typical radical of today does not think of himself as primarily a "worker": he reflects rather the disillusionment of a consumer-directed economy, the so-called affluent society. From his point of view, the looter who takes advantage of a race riot to steal a colour television set is a square and outmoded revolutionary. Again, political protest today tends to be sharply localized, and often takes the form of small ethnical solidarity movements, as with the separatism in Quebec, Belgium, Wales and Scotland. The primary revolutionary categories tend to be psychological rather than economic, closer in many respects to

Freud than to Marx. When the contemporary radical denounces intervention in Vietnam or Negro segregation, he does not think of these things as merely by-products of a class struggle, but as issues in which the moral and emotional factors, prejudice and the like, are the real enemies to be fought.

Such factors bring the radicalism of today closer to nineteenth-century anarchism than to the Communism of Stalin's era. Like the anarchists, contemporary radicals think in terms of direct action, or confrontation; and their organizing metaphor is not so much takeover as transformation or metamorphosis. Nineteenth-century anarchists showed a curious polarizing in temperament between the extremes of gentleness and of ferocity: there were the anarchists of "mutual aid", and the terrorist anarchists of bombs and assassinations. The essential dynamic of contemporary radicalism is non-violent, and its revolutionary tactics seem to descend from Gandhi rather than Lenin. When contemporary protest movements commit themselves to violence, they show some connexion with the fascism of a generation ago, a similarity which confuses many people of my generation, whose "left-wing" and "right-wing" signposts point in different directions. They feel turned around in a world where not only the Soviet Union but trade unions have become right-wing, and where many left-wing movements utter slogans that sound very close to racism.

Perhaps we should drop the metaphors of left and right wing, in a situation where we no longer have a conception of two parts of a society splitting off from each other and engaging in a final struggle for power. Radicals of today are still influenced by the metaphors of takeover, of which the phrase "student power" is one. But the context has changed: we should think rather of a single society, with a conservative majority and a number of radical groups embedded in it and trying to transform it from within. The aims and values of the conservative majority are not necessarily obscurantist, but are simply different. The epithet "conformist" is a double-edged one, for no social groups show more rigid patterns of conformity than nonconformist groups.

There is a strong feeling that it is the democracies of American and Western Europe which are most amenable to radical change today. If this is true, it is so only because the essential dynamic of the conservative majority in the democracies is also non-violent, forming the main body of a society mature and flexible enough to contain a good deal of organized opposition, including strikes. This implies that the first principle of the contest between radicals and conservatives in the democracies is not the principle of eventual struggle for power, but the principle of co-existence. Clearly, the one thing that would put an end to all hope for genuine social advance in our society would be the growth of conservative violence: the effort, with the aid of a hysterical police force, to trample down all protest into that state of uneasy quiescence under terror which is what George Wallace means by law and order. As the recent Chicago fracas showed, there can be no real doubt that such counter-violence would be much more directed at radicals, even of the most peaceful kind, than at criminals.

The dangers do not of course come entirely from the conservative side. Contemporary radical groups, including student activists, have in general no objective and documented analysis of what it is that they are against, such as Marx provided for Communists in *Das Kapital*. They are thus compelled to fall back on such cliché-phrases as "the establishment" or "power structure", which are used in a paranoid sense as implying a vast and vague conspiracy, much as "world bankers" and "international Jewry" were employed in fascist polemic. The danger here is that violence is often the only means of emotional release from a sense of unreality, in which even wantonly destructive or sadistic acts help to create a sense of identity in their perpetrators.

The real radical dynamic of our time, then, is not directed toward a once-for-all revolution which will transfer power from one class to another and then move on to a classless goal. It is rather a dynamic of permanent revolution (hardly in the old Trotskyist sense, I should think, though related), a dialogue of society engaged in a continuous critique of its order and its assumptions. Because of the central position it gives to the emotional and imaginative elements in radicalism, it can enlist those who are radical in other political areas, especially the artists. Old-line Marxism had a simple programme for writers and painters which was, in essence, protest before revolution, panegyric afterwards; and the prescriptions of "social realism" have been notoriously incapable of coming to terms with anything in twentieth-century culture which is genuinely revolutionary in form, and not merely in content.

In the radicalism of thirty years ago, the great disillusionment was the loss of belief in the moral superiority of the Soviet Union to the bourgeois world. The corresponding illusion of our own time is the belief in the possibility of achieving a moral superiority to society by withdrawing from it and its values, contemplating it from without as something alien, or, in the fashionable metaphor, "sick". When I call it an illusion I am not denying the possibility of human renewal: I am distinguishing between trying to preserve integrity, which is a genuine moral problem, and trying to preserve innocence, which is not one. It is easier to believe that a society which has been "sick" for thousands of years will get well immediately than to believe that we shall come to an immediate agreement on what constitutes health. The ethics of change can only be based on a paradoxical union of participation and detachment. We belong to something before we are anything, and what we belong to is a mixture of good and bad. At present students come to university demanding a greater degree of participation in its affairs, including its decisions. Given the conditions of our time, no reasonable person is likely to deny that this is a normal and healthy demand. But to participate in anything in human society means entering into a common bond of guilt, of guilt and of inevitable compromise. I am not saying that we accept the evils of what we join: I am saying that whatever we join contains evils, and that what we accept is the guilt of belonging to it.

The "commitment" and "engagement" we hear so much about are the preconditions of action, but they are not sufficent virtues, if they are virtues at all. Commitment in itself is uncritical and humorless: humorless because it is too busy rationalizing everything in what it belongs to to see the absurd side of it. We need also the opposition of detachment, which starts with a moral judgment on the social institution that one is in. I do not mean the token detachment of the opposition in a two-party political system, but a genuine detachment of attitude, one that keeps on saying: this, even if necessary, is still wrong; this, even if logical, is still absurd. In revolutionary times, however, what detachment is likely to do is to set up an alternative institution, which will of course also demand commitment. When this is set up in hostility to its conservative rival, that hostility is built into it, and so the commitment it calls for is of a more intense kind, more eager to rationalize, more impatient of having anomalies or absurdities in itself pointed out, less tolerant of dissent. Thus a revolutionary detachment from society may cancel itself out by a total commitment to another form of society, so that instead of getting more tolerance we eventually get less. We notice that educational experiments set up as part of a student protest often turn out to be more doctrinaire and narrow-minded than what they attempt to supersede, the fetishism of degrees and credits being replaced by the counter-fetishism of "revelance". A New York friend of mine tells me of a poster advertising a student-organized seminar in contemporary literature, set up as part of the Columbia demonstration, and ending with the statement: "Spokesmen of the so-called new criticism will not be tolerated".

Once a society renounces violence as a means of resolving its differences, controversy and discussion provide the only means of social advance. Where we have two separating camps of commitment, advance through discussion is paralyzed, because all arguments become personal. The argument is seen only as a rationalization of one side, and its proponent is merely identified as a radical or a reactionary, a Communist or an Uncle Tom. (I do not see much force in this last epithet, by the way: Uncle Tom, who was flogged to death for sticking by his principles, seems to me quite an impressive example of non-violent resistance.) The continuing of the paralysis of discussion, in breaking up meetings, shouting down unpopular speakers, and the like, congeals into a mood of anticipatory violence.

The end of commitment is the community; and commitment is what used to be called loyalty. Traditionally, loyalty is the acceptance of an external social authority, as embodied in nation or church or party or parents. It contains an uncritical element (e.g., "My country right or wrong"), and its ultimate sanction is power over life, as represented by the authority to draft young men to fight in Vietnam for a cause they may regard as foolish and evil. It seems clear that the sense of the rightness of this kind of loyalty is disappearing.

If the end of commitment is the community, the end of detachment is the individual. This is not an antithesis: the mature individual is mature only because he has reached a kind of social adjustment. The notion that individual freedom demands the destruction of all social order recurs in anarchist thought, but with much the same "by and by" feeling that the Christian has for the end of the world or the Communist for the withering away of the state. Such axioms as "anarchy is order", recently chalked up on London walls, do not seem to me any improvement on the "freedom is slavery" slogan of the police state in *1984*. We still need loyalty to something with enough authority to form a community, but it must be a *free* authority, something that fulfils and does not diminish the individual. Such an authority can ultimately only be the kind of authority that education embodies. The authority of the logical argument, the repeatable experiment, the established fact, the compelling work of art, is the only authority that exacts no bows or salutes. It is not sacrosanct, for what is true today may be inadequately true tomorrow, but it is what holds society together for today.

A century ago one of the most solidly rooted assumptions in our culture was the sense of continuity in time. History revealed an increasing purpose in its passing; consistency of action throughout life was what gave dignity to man and a real significance to his virtues, or even his vices. This belief in teleology, that time revealed a design and a meaning as it continued, had been built into our religion and philosophy from ancient times. It was still there in the arts of the last century, in the long novels that rolled through suspense and mystery to a foreordained conclusion, in the symphonies that took off from and returned to the same tonality, in the pictures that arrested a climactic point of process, like the self-portraits of Van Gogh or the poised dances of Dégas. This teleological sense is also disappearing. The word "absurd" refers to its disappearance, and to the growth of a feeling that all lives are really discontinuous moments of experience held together with various kinds of ideological paste. This loss of the sense of a future implicit in the present has naturally created a panic or latent hysteria, the future being feared in proportion to its meaninglessness. The panic about being up to date in one's cultural and intellectual vogues, and the panic about being taken over by some concealed and maleficent social design or "establishment", already mentioned, are aspects of this.

The real basis for this sense of the continuity of time was, I think, the sense of the continuity of social institutions. For centuries Western man has been enlarged and civilized essentially by his institutions: it was only the continuity of his nation, his church, his class, his party, his ancestry or his trade that gave his life a

dimension of greater significance. The loss of belief in the permanence of institutions, or rather in the assumption that they are any
better for being permanent, has brought us to a crisis of a peculiar
versatility. It is not a political or an intellectual or a religious crisis:
it is all these things at once, a crisis of the spirit unlikely to be
resolved by either revolution or reaction. Nothing new has been
born, yet at every moment we pass the point of no return. But it is
becoming clearer that social institutions are, in a sense, projected
from what man knows or imagines or wants to know, and which
are his arts and his sciences. The driving power of the continuity of
social institutions is the continuity of knowledge and of the learning process, and in a time when social projections no longer
command loyalty, we can only return to their source.

Meanwhile, the university is rooted in its society, a fact that
seems to have come as something of a discovery today, and not only
to students. There has been a good deal of discussion designed to
show that much of the attempt to define what Newman called the
idea of the university, in such phrases as "community of scholars",
is a smoke-screen for the university's involvement in a "sick"
society. A conference was held this summer under the title: "The
University: Rhetoric vs. Reality". It is no disparagement to the
usefulness of such a conference to say that rhetoric can never be
confronted by reality, but only by a different kind of rhetoric. In
any case the university is unlike most social institutions in that it is
committed to being aware of its social context, and to examining
the assumptions of its society. Some of the phrases used to indicate
this may be too idealistic to be convincing; but everthing connected
with the phrase "academic freedom" implies resistance to being
made a mere creature of the community. Thus the university is
precisely in the position of radical groups in modern society,
belonging to society yet striving to become aware of its conditioning, trying to throw off whatever is illegitimate in that conditioning, and therefore ethically bound to help carry out a long-term
transformation of society. Being an institution, it naturally regards
"confrontation" as a crisis and a last resort, not a series of rehear-
sals for an unwritten apocalyptic drama. And, of course, it may lose
the confrontation if it cannot resist legislative interference or economic pressure. But such defeats are the result of being in what we
have called the bond of guilt, the bond from which there is no
escape into innocence. Compromise is not a betrayal when a refusal to compromise would be a greater betrayal.

So far as the university is an institution, some proportioning of decision-making to the degree of commitment to it seems to me a reasonable principle: teaching staff and administration first, alumni with a lifelong record of work and interest in it second, students third. But the institutional aspect of the university exists only as a means of getting at the inner process of teaching and learning and scholarship, where the free authority of the subject is all that matters. A "child-centered" view of elementary education seems to me reasonable because those most concerned are children: a "student-centered" view of university education seems to me to be nonsense because university students are not children. They are citizens intelligent and mature enough to be brought into contact with the source of all continuity and structure in society, the bureau of standards where real time and space are kept.

There is another type of social institution which is also committed to the criticism of its social context and to an eventual transformation of society. This is the type represented by the religious bodies. It seems to me that some recognition of the role of religion in society is essential in clarifying today's radical protest, which is religious to a degree that it can hardly comprehend itself. Radicals today, in the universities particularly, are trying to find answers to the existential questions raised by discontinuity and absurdity, trying to solve the paradoxes resulting from the fact that man cannot live continuously on a genuinely human level. Such answers can only be sought in some area of religion, however secularized: they cannot be found in the university, which can deal only with the continuous and the structured. The religious bodies have enough problems of their own, but if they fail to meet the spiritual needs of society, the university will become the only source of free authority, and hence would be almost compelled to slip into the role of a lay church for intellectuals. That this would be a disaster, which could only widen the already dangerous gap between the intellectuals with their fragile opinions and the rest of society with its frightened police, goes without saying. I say it because many of the assumptions under which protest in the universities appears to be operating seem to me to take the form of a misapplied religious reformation, based on a view of the ideal university as a bastard church, resembling the Congregationalists in government, the Catholics in outlook, the Quakers in doctrine, and the Jehovah's Witnesses in tactics.

In revolutionary times the emotional emphasis is thrown on the break with the past; but the test of revolution comes with the problem of establishing contact with the past, when it can carry on as well as supersede. There are no immaculate conceptions in history, much less in the ethics of change. However new the future religions of Western man, they will still have to establish some contact with his Judaeo-Christian traditions; however new his future universities, they will still have to establish contact with the Western intellectual traditions that have come down from the Greeks. I spoke earlier of magical words, and at present no word is more magical than "dialogue", which raises the spirits of Socrates and Plato particularly. We notice in Plato however that the more dialogue there is, the more indecisive the discussion, and the greater the probability that somebody is talking nonsense. In this phase Socrates is the supreme ironist, breaking down and paralyzing all advance in the argument. But when any genuine knowledge is being conveyed, one person, generally Socrates himself, is on the trail of a dialectic, and is allowed to pursue it wherever it seems to lead, taking his followers with him. And, however breath-taking the myths and visions that we see on the way, over it all hangs the greater irony of the eventual martyrdom of Socrates, the fact that society as a whole can only absorb his influence by killing him. The spiritual tradition that runs through the Hebrew prophets and Jesus shows a similar pattern. In some of the protest of "yippies" and other groups today I detect a note of some desperation. Society does not hate them enough: they have not the prophetic authority to strike at our deeper fears, and are themselves involved in the panic they create. I imagine that we shall have to forge deeper loyalties, and confront deeper cleavages, if we are to follow our greatest teachers through an agony which is birth and death at once, to a victory which had triumphed over both.

Canada: New World Without Revolution

Canada, with four million square miles and only four centuries of documented history, has naturally been a country more preoccupied with space than with time, with environment rather than tradition. The older generation, to which I have finally become assigned, was brought up to think of Canada as a land of unlimited natural resources, an unloving but rich earth-mother bulging with endless supplies of nickel and asbestos, or, in her softer parts, with the kind of soil that would allow of huge grain and lumber surpluses. The result of such assumptions is that many of our major social problems are those of ecology, the extinction of animal species, the plundering of forests and mines, the pollution of water, as the hundreds of millions of years that nature took to build up our supplies of coal and oil are cancelled out in a generation or two. The archaeologists who explore royal tombs in Egypt and Mesopotamia find they are almost always anticipated by grave robbers, people who got there first because they had better reasons for doing so than the acquisition of knowledge. We are the grave robbers of our own resources, and posterity will not be grateful to us. There is, however, a growing understanding that our situation is not simply one of people against planes, or whatever the current issue may be, but of soil and trees and water against concrete and tarmac.

These spatial and environmental problems have a temporal dimension as well. Our history began in the seventeenth century, the age of Baroque expansion in Europe, where the countries advancing most rapidly into the future were those on the Atlantic seaboard. Rapid advance is usually followed either by rapid decline or by a rapid change in some other direction: even by then Spain and Portugal had passed their meridian of growth, and France soon turned back to its European preoccupations. If the French had held Canada they might well have sold it, as they did Louisiana. What is important is not nationality but cultural assumptions. The Baroque age was an age of intense belief in the supremacy of human consciousness over nature. It had discovered something of the technological potential of mathematics, once mathematics had become attached to a powerful social organization. It was not an age of individualism, as is often said, but an age of relatively enlightened despotism, and in some ways very like the dawn of civilization in the Near East, when the pyramids of Egypt and the ziggurats of Babylon emerged as dramatic witness to what men could do when united under a sufficiently strong social will. Both then and in the Baroque period mathematics, and the appearance of geometrical patterns in the human environment, was a symbol of aggressiveness, of imperialistic domination. We can see the results all over our country, in the grid patterns of our cities, the concession lines that divide up the farmland into squares, the railways and highways that emphasize direction through landscape rather than accommodation to it. Improvement in such communications always means a wider and straighter path through nature, and a corresponding decline of interest in it. With the coming of the aeroplane, even the sense of passing through a natural environment disappears. Our attitude to nature is reflected in our social environment, the kind we build ourselves. Washington was a city designed for automobiles rather than pedestrians long before there were any automobiles: Los Angeles, a city never designed at all, seems to have broken through the control even of the automobile. It was, after all, named after angels, who traditionally do not travel through space but simply manifest themselves elsewhere.

The religion that the British and French brought to the New World was not a natural monotheism, like the Algonquin worship of a Great Spirit, nor an imperial monotheism like that of the

Stoics, but a revolutionary monotheism, with a God who took an active and partisan role in history; and like all revolutionary movements, including Marxism in our time, it equipped itself with a canon of sacred books and a dialectical habit of mind, a mental attitude in which the neighboring heresy is much more bitterly hated than the total rejection of the faith. The dialectical habit of mind produced the conception of the false god, a conception hardly intelligible to an educated pagan. All false gods, in the Christian view, were idols, and all idolatry came ultimately from the belief that there was something numinous in nature. The Christian teaching was that there were no gods in nature; that nature was a fellow-creature of man, and that all the gods that had been discovered in it were devils. We have derived many benefits from this attitude, but it had a more sinister side: it tended to assume that nature, not being inhabited or protected by gods or potentially dangerous spirits, was simply something available for human exploitation. Everywhere we look today, we see the conquest of nature by an intelligence that does not love it, that feels no part of it, that splits its own consciousness off from it and looks at it as an object. The sense of the absolute and unquestionable rightness of man's conquest over nature extended to other cultures regarded as being in a "state of nature". The primary principle of white settlement in this country, in practice if not always in theory, was that the indigenous cultures should be destroyed, not preserved or continued or even set apart.

The spokesman for the Baroque phase of this attitude is Descartes, whose fundamental axiom, "I think, therefore I am," rested on a desire to derive human existence from human consciousness, and to see that consciousness as being in a different world from the nature which for Descartes was pure extension in space. This attitude, in itself a logical development from the traditional Christian view of nature, got so far away from idolatry that it became a kind of idolatry in reverse, the idol this time being human consciousness itself, separated from nature. We live today in a social environment which is a triumph of Cartesian consciousness; an abstract and autonomous world of interlocking co-ordinates, in which most of our imagination is focussed not on nature but on the geometrical shapes that we have imposed on nature. My own few childhood memories of big cities are full of a kind of genial clutter: crowds of people on streets, shops with their doors open, theatres with glittering lights; and certainly the exhilaration of this had much to do with the attractiveness of cities for those in smaller centres a generation or two ago. Much of it of course remains, but it is becoming clearer that each advance of technology is accompanied by an advance in introversion, and less sense of public use. Many of the streets now in these same cities, with their deserted sidewalks and cars whizzing up and down the road past scowling fortress-like buildings, show us the kind of anti-community symbolized for me by University Avenue in Toronto and by the areas in Los Angeles where pedestrians are regarded as vagrants. The amount of mental distress caused by living in an environment which expresses indifference or contempt for the perspectives of the human body is very little studied: one might call it proportion pollution.

My own university is in the middle of a big industrial city: this means great masses of box-lunch students, who commute in and out from distant suburbs and take their courses with little experience of a real university community, of the kind that Cardinal Newman regarded as the "idea" of the university. The surrounding streets keep steadily turning into anonymous masses of buildings that look eyeless in spite of being practically all windows. Many of them seem to have had no architect, but appear to have sprung out of their excavations like vast toadstools. City planners speak of the law of conserving the plan, meaning that Bloor Street in Toronto or Sherbrooke Street in Montreal are still where those streets originally were even though there has been a total metamorphosis of the buildings on them. But even this law, which seems at first sight like a concession to a sense of tradition, is really a means of confining change to the inorganic. And as we shuttle from a pigeon-hole in a high-rise apartment to another pigeon-hole in an office, a sense of futility and humiliation takes possession of us that we can now perhaps see in its historical dimension.

As civilization has "progressed" from axe to bulldozer, the growing withdrawal from nature paralyzes something natural in ourselves. A friend of my wife's, an interior decorator, remarked that she had a group of neurotic clients whom it seemed impossible either to please or to get rid of, and she suddenly realized that they had something in common: they all lived in high-rise apartments at a level above the trees. A withdrawal from nature extends into a growing withdrawal from human society itself. I mentioned the increasing introversion that technology brings with it: the aeroplane is more introverted than the train; the super-highway, where there is a danger of falling asleep, more introverted than the most unfrequented country road. The international airport, completely insulated even from the country it is in, is perhaps the most eloquent symbol of this, and is parodied in Stanley Kubrick's movie *2001*, where the hero lands on the moon, dependent on human processing even for the air he breathes, and finds nothing to do there except to phone his wife back on earth, who is out.

A revolutionary habit of mind, being founded on the sense of a crucial break in time at some point, the Exodus from Egypt, the Incarnation of Christ, the flight of Mohammed, the October Revolution in Russia, has a hostility to continuous tradition built into it. In Moslem countries everything that happened before Mohammed's time is part of the age of ignorance. Guides in developing countries, especially Marxist ones, want to show tourists the achievements of their own regime, and often get angry or contemptuous when the tourists want to see the cultural products of the old exploiting days. Similarly with our own culture. The Puritans in Massachusetts were in communion with the Puritans in Norwich who petitioned the Cromwellian government to pull down a useless and cumbersome cathedral which was a mere relic of superstition. Even the Jesuit missionaries, for all their zeal and devotion, still assumed that the Indians, so long as they were heathen, were a part of subconscious nature, and that only Christianity could incorporate them into a fully human society. A cultural sense thus got started which was still operative until quite recently. My late friend Charles Currelly, the founder of the Archaeological Museum in Toronto, was horrified by the indifference with which the authorities of his day regarded the British Columbia totem poles, and by the eagerness with which they were ready to sell them off to anyone whom they thought would be fool enough to want them. What we are now beginning to see is that an original belief in the rightness of destroying or ignoring a so-called "savage" culture develops toward a contempt for our own. In Margaret Atwood's very ironic novel *Surfacing*, the heroine, trying to get back to an original identity represented by the Quebec forest, finds that she has to destroy everything cultural that she possesses, or, as she says: "everything from history must be eliminated".

The revolutionary aspect of white settlement extended from religion into economics, as entrepreneur capitalism developed. Every technological change brought with it a large-scale shift in population centres. The skyline of Toronto sixty years ago was dominated by the spires of the great churches: now the churches are points of depression within the skyline. My moral is not the shift of interest from spiritual to financial administration: my moral is rather that the churches themselves are now largely without parishes, the population, at least the church-going part of it, having moved elsewhere. Similarly Canada is a land of ruins to an extent that the less spacious countries of Europe would not dare to be: ghost towns at exhausted mines or the divisional points of old railways remind us how quickly our economy can scrap not merely a building but an entire city. As Earle Birney remarks, the country is haunted by its lack of ghosts, for a ghost town has no ghosts: it is only one of the rubbish heaps that spring up in an economy of waste. We may remember Sam Slick on the beauties of Niagara Falls:

> "It would be a grand speck to get up a jint stock company for factory purposes, for such another place for mills ain't to be found atween the poles. Oh dear!" said I, "only think of the cardin' mills, fullin' mills, cotton mills, grain mills, saw mills, plaster mills, and gracious knows what sort o' mills might be put up there . . . and yet them goneys the British let all run away to waste."

For Sam Slick the ideal thriving mill town of this sort was Lowell in Massachusetts, where my father started in business, and it was a sad day for both us when I took him there as an old man, after all the mills had been moved to the south, and he saw only the empty shell of the town he once knew. One question that such events raise is obviously: what can or should be preserved of what is no longer functional, and has little interest in itself apart from being a part of our past?

Whatever the answer, our social environment is a revolutionary one in which the main forces are indiscriminately destructive. This has to some extent always been true. Once there was a great city called Nineveh, so great that, according to the Book of Jonah, it took three days to journey across it. Then, quite suddenly, Nineveh disappeared under the sand, where it remained for nearly three thousand years. This kind of destruction, from enemy action without, is a greater danger now, as hydrogen bombs would leave nothing for the sand to preserve; but along with it is the even more insidious sense of destruction from within, destruction that proceeds from the very nature of technology itself, not impossibly inspired by some deathwish in ourselves. The only possible economic alternative to capitalism, we feel, is socialism, but if capitalism is a destroyer, socialism is even more of one, because more committed to technology. In ancient Egypt one of the first things a new Pharaoh often did was to deface his predecessor's monuments: this is still our rhythm of life, but it is largely an unconscious one, except when rationalized as progress.

The violence of our almost unmanageable cities is bringing about another great population shift, as people move out of them and back to smaller centres. We are beginning to see a very large cycle of history turning here, and with this is slowly growing another social vision. Ecology, the sense of the need for conserving natural resources, is not a matter of letting the environment go back to the wilderness, but of finding some kind of working balance between man and nature founded on a respect for nature and its inner economies. As part of natural ecology, we are also developing some sense of the need for a kind of human ecology, of conserving not only our natural but our cultural and imaginative resources. Again, this is not simply a matter of leaving alone everything that is old: it is a way of life that grows out of a sense of balance between our present and our past. In relation to the natural environment, there are two kinds of people: those who think that nature is simply there to be used by man, and those who realize that man is himself a part of nature, and will destroy himself if he destroys it. In relation to time and human history, there are also two kinds of people: those who think that the past is dead, and those who realize that the past is still alive in us. A dead past left to bury its dead ends in a dead present, a society of sleepwalkers, and a society without a memory is as senile as an individual in the same plight.

The very word "preservation" reflects some of the panic that goes with the sense of imminent destruction. Some time ago Eric Arthur produced a book on Toronto called *No Mean City*, full of photographs of its older architecture. If we count the number of buildings that have been destroyed, many of them before the book appeared, we can see that there is something else in the city which is, if not mean, at least reckless and out of control, something that needs strong organizing to resist it. According to John Stuart Mill, there is a liberal and a conservative question to be asked about everything: what good is it? and why is it there? If these questions are asked about public, cultural or historical monuments, the prevailing answer in our day to the question, what good is it? is, no good unless useful to the present owner of the property it stands on; and the answer to the question, why is it there? is, because it is not yet worth anyone's while to remove it. Clearly we need more intelligible answers to both questions. What is called future shock is simply a by-product of the destructiveness of technology: it represents a genuine social problem, and it produces such mental diseases as the conviction among educators (noted by Bernie Hodgetts in hs trenchant survey of the teaching of Canadian history, *What Culture? What Heritage?*) that it doesn't matter what we teach, because society is so transient that all one's skills and assumptions will soon be out of date anyway. This is a lethal state of mind to get into. Trying to sharpen one's sense of the future is useless, as the future has no existence; trying to see the present as an interim in which anything may go at any time merely adds to the mood of destruction. Not everything that can happen will happen: we have to understand what kind of people we are before we can begin to guess what we shall do. What kind of people we are is perhaps determined, and certainly conditioned, by what we realize of our past, and sharpening our sense of the past is the only way of meeting the future. Preserving our heritage is a central part of that realization and that sharpened sense.

In the Book of Jeremiah there is an episode that I often return to, in which Jeremiah's secretary is reading, to the King of Judah, the prophecy which consists so largely of denunciations of the royal policy. A fire, we are told, was burning in the room, and every so often the infuriated king would cut off part of the scroll being read with a knife and throw it on the fire. This must have been a papyrus scroll, and what fascinates me is that the king's palace disappeared totally in a few years, and not the slightest trace of it remains, whereas the Book of Jeremiah, entrusted to the most fragile and combustible substance produced in the ancient world, is still with us, and still in reasonably good shape. The inference, or at least the human inference, appears to be that what is easiest to preserve is what has the power of reproduction. Literature has always survived much better than the visual arts for this reason, and now, with recorded music, photography, and tape, an immense amount of cultural material has become preservable. From the Avalon peninsula to the Queen Charlotte Islands, scholars have been collecting ballads, folksongs, folktales, and whatever a tape recorder can preserve of vanishing attitudes and ways of life. Sometimes the collector arrives too late for the crucial things to be preserved, but what is done is better than nothing, and our archives and libraries are growing in cultural importance accordingly. One of the most rewarding of the WPA projects of forty years ago was the Index of American Design, an inventory of the conventions of the popular visual arts, a project which extended into Canada, and this kind of record is still one of our most useful allies in the fight against oblivion.

As part of this development, the contempt for primitive or popular art that so distressed Currelly a half-century ago has largely disappeared: in fact we set so high a value now on such art that we have almost transformed the Eskimos into a nation of sculptors, at least with one hand, even though we may be destroying the sources of their creativeness with the other. Some of our attitude to this, perhaps can be discounted as a patronizing sense of what used to be called the "picturesque", something which appeals to us because we think it comes just under our own standard of sophistication. But this is a minor and expendable attitude: what really attracts us in what we so misleadingly call "primitive" art is rather the recognition of a powerful convention at work within it. Such a convention is in the visual arts something of a parallel to what the ability to reproduce is in literature: it indicates, if it does not guarantee, a continuing vitality in the tradition that will make possible a steady production of high quality. Similar conventions operate, or should operate, in the area generally called handicraft, but the one-sided competition with mass-produced goods has largely reduced this to a boutique culture, or what I think of as the ashtray syndrome. In the past, everything from buildings to clothes and household objects went through a certain cycle of taste: first they were in fashion, then they fell out of fashion and became ridiculous; then they settled into the softer lighting of "quaint", and cultivated people became interested in them again, and finally they began to take on some of the archaic dignity of the primitive. Nowadays, the expanding of the antique market and the growing sense of the possible commercial value of whatever is no longer being produced has considerably shortened this process. The sojourn in a period of unfashionable limbo has to be very brief when an "antique" can be an object twenty years old. Similarly, immigrants from Europe or Asia often reject their own cultural heritage in an effort to adapt to the new country, so that it takes another generation before they turn toward their own origins again, but that cycle is also shortening.

This levelling out of cultural interest is in itself healthy: the wild fluctuations of taste and fashion in the past have done nothing but harm, and any philosophy of preservation has to avoid the value-judgments which are really nothing but rationalizings of a destructive impulse. I think of the Italian Director of Antiquities in Thornton Wilder's *The Cabala*, whose reputation was based on his eagerness to destroy a Baroque church in order to expose a thirteenth-century door. Our attitude to the past needs more of the impartiality of the archaeologist who excavates all layers and cultural periods of his site with equal care. One would be very deficient in imagination and curiosity not to have some interest in relics of the Hopewell culture or in the Norse remains, if that is what they are, at L'Anse aux Meadows in Newfoundland. But the industrial archaeology that uncovers the pottery, glass and brick factories of nineteenth-century Ontario has its importance too, as we need more tangible reminders of our immediate past than the mere fact that many place-names end in "mills".

Despite the best efforts of reproduction, it remains true that any physical artefact is subject to decay, especially if it is an outdoor object in any climate that at all resembles ours. Restoration is an often disastrous solution: tourists in English cathedrals hear a good deal about the vandalism of Cromwell's soldiers, but the devastation wrought by Victorian restorers has been often far worse, however much better the motive. The kind of preservation that we have in Williamsburg and similar large-scale open museums is in a sense almost anti-historical: it shows us, not life in time as a continuous process, but life arrested at a certain point, in a sort of semi-permanent drama. There is nothing wrong with this, but it gives us a cross-section of history, a world confronting us rather than preceding us. Something similar is true of the building which is a historical allusion or quotation, like collegiate Gothic, replicas of European churches, or Georgian residential areas. The tendency to make the past contemporary with the present is part of what Shakespeare means when he says, addressing Time:

> Our dates are brief, and therefore we admire
> What thou dost foist upon us that is old,
> And rather make them born to our desire,
> Than think that we before have heard them told.

In a sense every physical artefact is a protest against time, an expression of a desire for permanence in a world of change. This is especially true of the huge monuments put up by kings, priests and dictators, either to their own glory or to the glory of their gods or nations. We notice a persistent association between such monuments and death, and from the pyramids to our own war memorials there has run the constant realization that death is the nearest that life can get to permanence. One of the better chapters in *Parkinson's Law* remarks on the tendency of institutions to put up their largest and most impressive buildings at the moment when they are passing out of existence, so that the building instantly becomes a kind of cenotaph. In a national capital like Ottawa, one could perhaps think of more examples than it would be tactful to mention. In general, the kind of, artefact that posterity usually finds the most expendable culturally is also the hardest to remove physically.

In every age great artists attach themselves to the social establishment, and make their living from it, or, at least, live without questioning or quarrelling with it. Many of the artists we most deeply revere today, Bach, Shakespeare, Michelangelo, were busy professional men with commissions to fill and deadlines to meet. And yet, as time goes on, this view of culture, in which the artists are dependent on the patronage of their societies, begins to reverse its perspective. In nearly forty years of teaching literature in a university, I have found that William Morris is a writer and artist whose interest for me has never palled, and whose influence on my own social attitude has remained central. In Morris there is an apparent inconsistency between his fascination with medieval culture and his very left-of-centre political views. The inconsistency disappears when we realize that for Morris the creators of a culture, and those who give it its style, are not warriors or kings or priests, or the political or religious ideas they stand for, but architects and sculptors and poets. The ideal world that he presents in *News from*

Nowhere is a world where everyone has become something of an artist, though it is the quality of design in the so-called minor or functional arts that he is primarily interested in, and regards as the essential clue to a culture's vitality. Morris' future world is not very interested in history or in preserving its past: it is too happy designing and making things in the present, though there is an indication at the end of the story that its historical perspective is going to expand. But even without this indication Morris makes an important point for those who do wish to preserve their past. Our sense of the need for preservation has in it a certain distrust in the integrity of our own cultural tradition: once things are gone, we have little confidence in our ability to replace them with new things equally good. The trouble is, once again, not the lack of creative people, but the lack of response to creativeness in our society. The rudder, so to speak, that guides our philosophy of preservation ultimately has to be the continuing vitality of our cultural tradition. Without that, the task of preserving our heritage will have in it a quality of desperation unhealthy both for it and for us.

Our museums preserve objects of the past, and by preserving them, if William Morris is right, they also express a potentially revolutionary view of history. I spoke earlier of the developing countries who are so proud of the achievements of their own regime and so impatient with the culture of their reactionary past. Even in China, deeply interested as it is in archaeology, a friend of mine, inspecting some of the great cultural monuments of Peking a few years ago, was accompanied by a guide who remarked that if she had her way she would cover them all up with posters explaining how badly exploited the workers were in those days. The point is, I think, that the social milieu of any culture will always be full of human folly and cruelty, but that whatever is beautifully designed always remains in the state of innocence, always a symbol of the kind of thing that human struggles for freedom and happiness are about.

In a sense it is a considerable advantage to Canada not to have so much history to live with as the European countries, to say nothing of the Middle Eastern ones. In so small and thickly settled a country as England, archaeology has to be largely a salvaging operation, a matter of keeping one jump ahead of the steam shovel.

There is no way out of this, short of an atomic war that would cut the world's population in half, and in the meantime the preservation of visible monuments has its own kind of panic. However strongly we may condemn Henry VIII's dissolution of the monasteries, it might have been a crushing burden for the National Trust if all those abbeys had survived. Similarly, it is exceptional when the actual site of an important or interesting event, like the murder of Becket in Canterbury Cathedral, still remains: most of what historical markers remind us of has vanished forever into Newtonian space. Here again what is of primary importance is the quality of our historical imagination, the ability, if I may try to express something very difficult to express, to see things, not merely as objects confronting us, but as growing in time, as having come out of our own past and moving towards our own future.

The title of my talk speaks of Canada as a new world without revolution. As you have gathered, there is a certain irony in this: we have fully participated in all the social and cultural consequences of the American revolution, and its advantages and disadvantages are equally ours. Even Quebec, so long preoccupied with maintaining the traditions of its past, has gone through a remarkably complete cultural revolution, though alleged to be a quiet one. Yet it is still perhaps the absence of a revolutionary tradition in Canada, the tendency to move continuously rather than discontinuously through time, that has given Canadian culture one very important and distinctive characteristic. This is its respect for the documentary. Canadian painting began with documentary painters like Krieghoff and Paul Kane, who may have kept an eye on the European market but were nevertheless keen observers of what was around them. Group of Seven painting, along with that of Thomson and Emily Carr, was documentary painting to an unusual degree, almost an imaginative mapping and survey of the remoter parts of the country; and we have also the extensive "war records" of painting from both wars. What Jackson and Thomson did for landscape Riopelle and Pellan and their contemporaries are doing for the Cartesian culture that we live in now. Canadian film has always been remarkable for its sensitive documentary feeling, applied to everything from Eskimo and Indian life to the urban cultures of Toronto and Montreal. Canadian literature, in the nineteenth century as well as this one, and in both poetry and fiction, has had a distinctive attachment to a sober narrative technique, a clear sense of fact, and a curious tendency to itemize, to make a functional use of lists and catalogues and inventories. The implication is, perhaps, that the Canadian consciousness is one peculiarly adapted to preserving its own heritage, not like a miser guarding his hoard or a watchdog snarling at a burglar, not like a man living among his memories and reshaping them in a form more attractive to his ego, but like one who understands that all coherent action, as well as all moral integrity, depends on the continuity of the present with the past.

The Rear-View Mirror: Notes Toward A Future

I have been called, very generously, a scholar, and ideally there is no difference between a scholar and a teacher. But in practice there is a good deal of difference, at least in emphasis. I think all my books have been teaching books rather than scholarly books: I keep reformulating the same central questions, trying to put them into a form to which some reader or student will respond: "Yes, now I get it". A more typical scholar than I, I should think, can be much more of a guru: he can train other scholars; he is at his best in the graduate school, and when his students become scholars in their turn, they have his brand mark, so to speak, printed on them. I teach mainly undergraduates, and I find the undergraduate classroom important for my writing. And yet the teacher-student relation, as such, seems to me a curiously embarrassing one: I want my students released from it as soon as possible to go and do their own thing. Their own thing may very well by teaching, of course; but what interests me even more is the great variety of things that students in an undergraduate classroom go on to do. Because this is what indicates most clearly the variety of ways that the university affects the society it belongs to.

I recently read an article, written by someone much younger than myself, which said sternly that the twentieth century is moving so fast that anyone born when I was, in 1912, is at best a survivor from an earlier age, a dinosaur who may not realize how cold it's getting. But it has been often pointed out that Canada itself is peculiarly a land of survival: a huge loosely assembled collection of territories, divided by language, geography and politics, can only stay together by constantly meeting a series of crises, each of them carrying the threat of not surviving if the crisis is not met. So perhaps Canada has something in common with my generation. During the sixty-odd years that Canada and I have survived together, it seems to me that Canada has become steadily more typical of the world it is in. Survival in itself is nothing to be complacent about: people survive a war only because other people do not; and if we worry less about nuclear destruction than we did, it is because the worry is intolerable, not because the threat is any less of a threat. But the survival of society as a whole is usually considered a good thing: we may be surviving in a fool's paradise, but perhaps no other paradise is appropriate for human beings.

If I can believe what that article said, along with so many others that say much the same thing, the world I was born into in 1912 was both a stable world and a simple one, a world of ordered values, whereas now these values are being questioned or denied, and are either disappearing or turning into something else. People of my generation, in short, were brought up to be against sin and in favour of motherhood, and can't cope with a world where motherhood is out and sin is in. Being a literary critic, when I am faced with statements like this I look first at the literary conventions behind them, and then at the metaphors they use. The convention is what critics call a pastoral myth, and it descends from ancient stories of lost gardens of Eden and vanished golden ages. Pastoral myths are mostly illusions projected from the experience of growing older. A child's world seems simple and innocent to the adult, so he assumes that the world as a whole was simpler when he was a child, and by extension even simpler before that. But however natural this assumption may be it is clearly nonsense: there have never been any simple ages.

As for the metaphors, what they really say is: the world used to be solid; now it's liquid. The basis for these metaphors is chiefly money: if we can put a dollar into a bank with a reasonable hope of still having a dollar when we take it out again, then our world looks solid, and all our social, political and religious values look solid too. Rapid inflation makes the world liquidate very quickly, and we have to live from one moment to the next by a combination of faith and self-hypnotism, like the people in the Far East who walk over hot coals, to the great bewilderment of tourists, most of whom are capable of self-hypnotism but not of faith.

What I am talking about is what is often called future shock, the sense of uneasiness caused by a technology moving faster than the human ability to control it. This is also a standard myth, the story of the sorcerer's apprentice, the machine that could be started but not stopped. Uneasiness about the future is there, certainly, and the basis for it is real enough; but I have no expertise in this area. What I hope I do know something about starts with the fact that there is no such thing as future shock, because nobody knows one instant of the future, except by analogy with the past.

Metaphors are tricky things to handle. We think we know that the earth revolves around the sun, but we still say "sunrise" and "sunset" because we don't really believe it. The sun revolves around the world that concerns us, and doubtless always will. Similarly, if we're driving a car, we look ahead of us to see where we're going, but what applies to moving in space doesn't apply to moving in time. We move in time with our backs to what's ahead and our faces to the past, and all we know is in a rear-view mirror. But we don't like to think this way: we say to a young person: "you have a great future ahead of you", and forget what we mean is: "you will probably have a good deal more past to contemplate". The humanities are often reproached with their concern over the past, but there is no difference between the humanities and any other form of knowledge on this point. The humanities change just as radically as the sciences do, and on the same principles. There is nothing new under the sun except our knowledge of what is under the sun, but that new knowledge is a constant recreation of old knowledge.

The question "Where are we going?" assumes that we already know the answer to the question "Where are we now, and how did we get here?". We certainly don't know the answer to that one, and in fact all our really urgent, mysterious and frightening questions have to do with the burden of the past and the meaning of tradition. Here we are in Canada, confronted with so many problems that demand immediate solution. Nobody denies their importance, but what continues to fascinate us is the reinterpreting of our history. What seems really important to us is that all Canadians don't agree with the British North America Act of a century ago, or about the Quebec Act a century before that. Oh well, we say, that's just Canada, always fussing about its identity, like a neurotic who can't deal with the world until he's got his private past unsnarled. But it isn't just Canada: there's the weight of a past of slavery on emerging nations in Africa, the weight of the British Empire on contemporary Britain, of the Old Testament on Israel, of Marxist doctrine on the Soviet Union. Up to the Vietnam war, more or less, many people in the United States believed that the American way of life had only to progress and look ahead: their view of life for themselves was based on the car-driving metaphor. But now most Americans also, I think, regard their past as something in front of them to be studied, not behind them to run away from.

I understand the fear that our civilization will fail to adapt in time to the changes which its technology has already started. But the word "adapt" may be misleading, because there is no environment to adapt to except the one we have created. Man is the one animal that has stopped playing the Darwinian game of adaptation, and has tried to transform the environment instead. Much of his transformation so far has been pollution, waste, overcrowding and destruction, and there is a limit beyond which he can't go on doing this. At least I hope there's a limit: there are movies like *Star Wars* which suggest that we can learn to visit distant galaxies and smash them up too; but I'd prefer not think of that as our future.

The American poet Wallace Stevens wrote a poem called "Description Without Place", in which he says that man does not live directly in the world, he lives inside his own constructs of that world. Nothing like nationality has any existence in nature, and yet, Stevens says, when we are in Spain everything looks Spanish. A parallel of latitude divides Canada from the United States; a meridian of longitude, Manitoba from Saskatchewan. Such things don't exist in the world of birds and trees, of course; but on the other hand, the world of birds and trees doesn't exist for us, except as part of the constructed human world which starts with things like Canada and its provinces.

I have spent most of my professional life studying one aspect of the way man constructs the world he lives in; the aspect I call a mythology, the building of worlds out of words. Nobody can create, think or even act outside the mythology of his time, but a mythology is not some kind of prison; it is simply the whole body of verbal material we work with. Like science, it is being recreated all the time, partly by critics and scholars and partly by literature itself, because every new writer recreates something already in literature. So anyone teaching literature gets involved with mythology, and this very quickly carries him past the boundaries of literature into the social function of words.

In forty years of teaching, I have never seen any differences among my students, as students, that could be ascribed to sex or ethnical origin. But of course I see any amount of social conditioning, in every classroom I go into. Gradually it dawns on a teacher of English that he is in contact with the student's total verbal experience, and that probably less than one per cent of that experience has been derived from anything that he would call literature. The rest is made up of social conditioning, from television and other news media, casual conversations, advertising, the chattering of the student's own subconscious, and so on. All teachers know that their students need to become aware of and question their assumptions; but perhaps the teacher of English sees most clearly how militant a job teaching is, and what kind of enemy it has to fight. What faces him is not simply a mass of unexamined assumptions but a complete and mostly phony mythology, made up of cliché and prejudice and stock response, a kind of parody of the one he is trying to teach.

We think of reading as essential to living in a modern society, which of course it is. But in itself it only attaches us to that society; it doesn't set us free from it. In the subway, where I do a certain amount of my writing, I can see around me four signs telling me not to do things, three sets of instructions about what to do in an emergency, and two threats of fine or imprisonment if there turns out not to be any emergency. There is also a long document in fine print I have never read, besides all the advertising. It's clear that the primary motive for teaching one to read is to produce an obedient and adjusted citizen, who can respond to a traffic sign with the right reflex. This conformity is probably the only basis for living in a complicated society: we belong to something before we are anything, and the individual grows out of the group, not the other way round. There is nothing much wrong with the fact that most students are conformists, including of course the rebellious students, who are bigoted conformists. But social adjustment is a beginning, not an end, and on this basis of conformity the teacher has to work for their liberal education, trying to transfer their loyalties from ready-made responses to the real world of human constructive power. As the university comes very late in a student's life, the teacher may have to work only with a few, but that few makes all the difference in the level of the civilization it belongs to.

How is it that people get trapped in phony mythologies? As Thomas Pynchon says in his novel *Gravity's Rainbow*, man is a paranoid animal, always claiming that the world he's made is the real world, and that it's the order of God or of nature, or both, as well. This means, in reverse, that there can't be any reality that doesn't have an essential relation to us. The notion that God made the world primarily for the sake of man was built into our religious consciousness for centuries. What other point could there possibly be in making the world? people asked, without realizing how sick their question was. It was a slow and painful adjustment to seeing the world as a place that got along for millions of years without man, and still could, in fact still may. Or else we claim that what we impose on our world is what nature put there. When we had a society with "nobles" on top and "commoners" below, people tended to assume that those on top had "noble blood", and were better by birth or nature than the others.

Such constructs are at first partial: in early times one nation would assume that it had supreme rights over the rest of the world; another nation would make the same assumption, so they would go to war, and the winner was the one who was right. But as human life has slowly expanded over the whole globe, it has become steadily clearer that all enemies, proletariats, slaves, scapegoats and second-class people are products of illusion, things to be outgrown, and the longer we cling to such illusions, the more obviously evil and disastrous our attachment to them becomes. St. Paul reminded the Athenians that there is only one human race: I say reminded, because he clearly assumed that it was a fact they would know. We know it too, but are very unwilling to act on it: however, there are signs that we are making a beginning. Some of us have even begun to wonder whether the world of animals and plants, perhaps also of coal and oil deposits, really exists only for our benefit.

Every classroom shows a division between those who take in what education is about and those who stay with cliché and stock response. This creates a distinction that I would call the distinction between concern and anxiety. Concern is the response of the adult citizen to genuine social problems. Anxiety is based on the desire to exclude or subordinate, to preserve the values or benefits of society for the group of right people who know the right answers. The anxieties closest to teaching the humanities, I suppose, are those of prudery and propriety, or what I think of as garrison anxieties, the desire to keep everyone in parade uniform so that it will be easy to distinguish the officers.

One of the more attractive features of my own life in Toronto has been in seeing many anxieties of this type gradually relaxed, or even abandoned. In my younger days there was a great deal of anxious deference paid to women, of a kind that was clearly connected with keeping them out of many fields of social activity. There were anxieties about the freedom of expression claimed by painters and sculptors, and art galleries resounded with comparisons to what one's five-year-old kid could do. There were frantic anxieties about sexual scenes or four-letter words in books: the copy of *Ulysses* that I am still using was smuggled in to me from Buffalo by a friend. When I was a student, a young woman in a Latin class who had memorized the crib went on placidly translating a passage of Horace which the anxious editor had removed from the text to safeguard her purity, and I have never forgotten the vision of futility that that opened up for me. Religious bodies cultivated special kinds of anxiety, and felt that it increased their virtue to do so. Jokes that assumed racial or sexual or class prejudice abounded, and the assumptions in them were more or less taken for granted. And a policewoman set up as a sexual decoy could hardly be festooned with more warnings and special instructions than those surrounding the purchase of liquor.

Nevertheless, Toronto went on expanding from an uptight Scotch-Irish town to a cosmopolitan city, with art galleries and theatres and bookshops presenting a kind of imaginative experience that fifty years ago would have filled the newspapers with screams of panic and despair. I know that all this is only a normal part of a big city's growth; I am merely saying that it has been rather exhilarating to live through. I know too that no dragon ever dies: many people feel that their security is bound up with their anxieties, and Canadian novelists even yet are struggling with the same kind of hysteria that faced Morley Callaghan half a century ago. It may be thought too that many of these things are rather trivial. I happen not to think so. It's the job of a teacher of the humanities to keep fighting for the liberalizing of the imagination, to encourage students to confront experience, to explore the shadows and the darkness, to distinguish evil from the portrayal of evil, and to meet the unexpected with tolerance. If I am right, this is a fight on the front line of social good will, an aspect of what in religion is called charity.

The democratic ideal is one of equality, where everyone has the same rights before the law, but not, except indirectly, one of freedom. It tries to provide the conditions of freedom, but freedom itself is an experience, not a condition, and only the individual can experience it. So for freedom there has to be some tension between society and the individual. As the democracies have continued to maintain this tension, another movement has begun to take shape, which I think may be the most significant social movement of our time. This is the rise of the small community that coheres around a cultural tradition. For culture, in contrast to political and economic movements, tends to decentralize: it is usually based on a distinctive language, which is one of the most fragmented forms of human expression, and its products, like fine wines, are restricted to a small area in growth, if not in appeal.

In the world around us there are, first, the colonies of the old empires which have come to independence, and are now looking for their own cultural traditions. Then there are the small ethnic groups that have refused to be entirely assimilated to larger ones, like the Welsh in Britain or the Bretons in France. Some of these groups have a long history of oppression and repression, and partly because of this they may include violent or terroristic elements. These are naturally the ones we get to hear most about, but they are not the really significant ones, because violence always brings about the opposite of what it aims at. The extent to which political separation may be necessary for a culture will vary with circumstances, and often it may be simply the result of clinging to obsolete patterns of thinking. The centralizing political and economic movements have built up huge cities; these cities are now

almost unmanageable, and I think a decentralizing cultural movement is likely to become more dominant. But I think as it goes on it
will also become less political.

In every part of Canada there are strong separatist feelings,
some political, as in Quebec, some economic, as in the west, some
geographical, as in the Maritimes. But the genuine movement
underlying all this is a feeling of cultural distinctiveness, and this,
I think, will keep breaking down into smaller units as more of the
country becomes articulate. In the last fifteen years or so, I have
noticed how an increasing number of writers and painters in
Canada have come to regard the place where they are living not as
an accident, but as an environment that nourishes them, and
which they in turn bring into articulateness. We speak of American
literature, but what we have are mainly Mississippi writers, New
England writers, Parisian expatriate writers, southern California
writers. Similarly, I think Canadian literature will become more
and more a literature of regions. It seems to be a cultural law that
the more specific the setting of literature is, the more universal its
communicating power.

One reason why this movement interests me is that it could
give the university a social function which would be its traditional
function renewed. The reason why I have stayed in the university is
very largely the fact that I have never got over the impact of my four
undergraduate years. As an undergraduate, I was in a small community of students concerned mainly with the liberal arts. This
was a community in which life could be experienced with a far
greater intensity than anywhere else, because it was a life in which
the intellect and the imagination had a functional role to play. It is
no good arguing with me, or with anyone else who has had a
similar experience, about the practical value of spending four years
at university. The experience is its own value, and is a totally
irreplaceable one. Modern universities have been geared to political and economic expansion: they have developed into multiversi-
ties, with research institutes and professional training centres. As a
result systems of financing have grown up that are based on size,
and have practically compelled the universities to compete for
students and to suggest that degrees were essential for a better job or
social position. We still need research institutes and professional
training schools: the question is whether they should be set up in
such a way as to smother one of the real centres of university life. I

would hope to see the small university community come into focus again as the spark plug of a small cultural area that was beginning to feel its own articulateness.

I began by saying that the rear-view mirror is our only crystal ball: there is no guide to the future except the analogy of the past. But one's view of the past is coloured by prejudice and narrowed by ignorance, and so the future, when it comes to join the past, is always unexpected. Many people base their lives on what they think of as the future: the writer hopes he will be read in the future if he is neglected at present; the radical dreams of a revolutionary future and the conservative of a safeguarded one. I have my hopes of the future too, but future generations are never the children of light: they are no better than those they followed, though they see different things. One is wiser to leave the future to itself: whatever else it may do, it will not fulfil our hopes in the way we anticipate. But as our personal future narrows, we become more aware of another dimension of time entirely, and may even catch glimpses of the powers and forces of a far greater creative design. Perhaps when we think we are working for the future we are really being contained in the present, though an infinite present, eternity in an hour, as Blake calls it. Perhaps too that present is also a presence, not an impersonal cause in which to lose ourselves, but a person in whom to find ourselves again. Thou art that, as the Hindus say. If the selection committee feels that I have done anything to improve the lot of mankind, I am of course very pleased. There is another kind of pleasure, however, in feeling that even in its accidents, whether of suffering or of triumph, a human life may not be "lot" at all, but a life that because it dies is a real life, a freedom that because it is known and determined is once and always free.

Acknowledgements

1. "Culture as Interpenetration," an address read to UNESCO's International Council of Philosophy and Humanistic Studies, Montreal, Canada, September 16, 1977.

2. "Across the River and Out of the Trees," from *University of Toronto Quarterly*, vol. 50, no. 1 (Fall 1980) and *The Arts in Canada: The Last Fifty Years*, edited by W.J. Keith and B.-Z. Shek, pp. 1-14 ©University of Toronto Press 1980. Reprinted by permission of University of Toronto Press.

3. "National Consciousness in Canadian Culture," an address read to the Royal Society of Canada, June 7, 1976. Reprinted in the *Transactions of the Royal Society*, Series IV, vol. XIV, 1976, pp. 57-69. Reprinted by permission of the author.

4. "Sharing the Continent," from "Canadian Culture Today," an address read to the "Twentieth Century Canadian Culture Symposium," Washington, D.C., February 2, 1977.

5. "Conclusion" to the *Literary History of Canada: Canadian Literature in English*, Second Edition, ed. Carl Klinck. vol. III, pp. 318-332 (University of Toronto Press, 1976). Reprinted by permission of the author.

6. "Teaching the Humanities Today," from "The Presidential Address," delivered at the 91st annual convention of the Modern Language Association in New York City, December 27, 1976. Reprinted in *PMLA*, vol. 92, no. 3 (May 1977), pp. 385-91. Reprinted by permission of the Modern Language Association of America.

7. "Humanities in a New World," an address delivered for the installation of Claude Bissell as President of the University of Toronto, November 22, 1958. Published by the University of Toronto Press (Toronto, 1959), pp. 9-23. Reprinted by permission of University of Toronto Press.

8. "The Writer and the University," from "Culture and the National Will," Convocation Address, Carleton University, May 17, 1957. Published by Carleton University for the Institute of Canadian Studies (Ottawa, 1957). Reprinted by permission of the Institute of Canadian Studies.

9. "The Teacher's Source of Authority," an address read at the American Educational Research Association Conference, March 30, 1978. Published in *Curriculum Inquiry Journal* 9:1 (New York: John Wiley & Sons, 1979), pp. 3-11. Copyright © 1979, Ontario Institute for Studies in Education. Reprinted by permission of John Wiley & Sons.

10. "The Definition of a University," a lecture at the Ontario Institute for Studies in Education, November 4, 1970. Published in *Alternatives in Education: OISE Fifth Anniversary Lectures,* ed. Bruce Rusk (Toronto: General Publishing Company), pp. 71-90. Reprinted by permission of the Ontario Institute for Studies in Education.

11. "The Ethics of Change," an address given at Queen's University, Kingston, Ontario, November 8, 1968. Published in *The Ethics of Change: A Symposium* (Toronto: Canadian Broadcasting Corporation, 1969), pp. 44-55. Reprinted by permission of the CBC.

12. "Canada: New World Without Revolution," an address given at the Royal Society Symposium, October 7, 1975. Published in *Preserving the Canadian Heritage* for the Royal Society of Canada in 1975, pp. 15-25. Reprinted by permission of the author.

13. "The Rear-View Mirror," from an address read on the occasion of the Royal Bank Award, Toronto, Ontario, September 18, 1978.

Index